Lecture Notes
in Business Information Processing

371

Series Editors

Wil van der Aalst
RWTH Aachen University, Aachen, Germany
John Mylopoulos
University of Trento, Trento, Italy
Michael Rosemann
Queensland University of Technology, Brisbane, QLD, Australia
Michael J. Shaw
University of Illinois, Urbana-Champaign, IL, USA
Clemens Szyperski
Microsoft Research, Redmond, WA, USA

More information about this series at http://www.springer.com/series/7911

Dietmar Winkler · Stefan Biffl ·
Daniel Mendez · Johannes Bergsmann (Eds.)

Software Quality

Quality Intelligence in Software and Systems Engineering

12th International Conference, SWQD 2020
Vienna, Austria, January 14–17, 2020
Proceedings

 Springer

Editors
Dietmar Winkler 🆔
Vienna University of Technology
Vienna, Austria

Stefan Biffl 🆔
Vienna University of Technology
Vienna, Austria

Daniel Mendez 🆔
fortiss GmbH, Germany,
and Blekinge Institute of Technology
Karlskrona, Sweden

Johannes Bergsmann
Software Quality Lab GmbH
Linz, Austria

ISSN 1865-1348   ISSN 1865-1356 (electronic)
Lecture Notes in Business Information Processing
ISBN 978-3-030-35509-8   ISBN 978-3-030-35510-4 (eBook)
https://doi.org/10.1007/978-3-030-35510-4

This Springer imprint is published by the registered company Springer Nature Switzerland AG
The registered company address is: Gewerbestrasse 11, 6330 Cham, Switzerland

Message from the General Chair

The Software Quality Days (SWQD) conference and tools fair was first organized in 2009 and has since grown to be the largest yearly conference on software quality in Europe with a strong and vibrant community. The program of the SWQD conference was designed to encompass a stimulating mixture of practice-oriented presentations, scientific presentations of new research topics, tutorials, and an exhibition area for tool vendors and other organizations in the area of software quality.

This professional symposium and conference offers a range of comprehensive and valuable opportunities for advanced professional training, new ideas, and networking with a series of keynote speeches, professional lectures, exhibits, and tutorials.

The SWQD conference welcomes anyone interested in software quality including: software process and quality managers, test managers, software testers, product managers, agile masters, project managers, software architects, software designers, requirements engineers, user interface designers, software developers, IT managers, release managers, development managers, application managers, and many more.

The guiding conference topic of the SWQD 2020 was "Quality Intelligence: Software Quality in the Absence of Well-Defined Requirements," as changed product, process, and service requirements, e.g., distributed engineering projects, mobile applications, involvement of heterogeneous disciplines and stakeholders, extended application areas, and new technologies include new challenges and might require new and adapted methods and tools to support quality assurance activities early.

January 2020   Johannes Bergsmann

Message from the Scientific Program Chairs

The 12th Software Quality Days (SWQD) conference and tools fair brought together researchers and practitioners from business, industry, and academia working on quality assurance and quality management for software engineering and information technology. The SWQD conference is one of the largest software quality conferences in Europe.

Over the past years, we received a growing number of scientific contributions to the SWQD symposium. Starting back in 2012, the SWQD symposium included a dedicated scientific program published in scientific proceedings. In this ninth edition, we received an overall number of 17 high-quality submissions from researchers across Europe which were each peer-reviewed by 3 or more reviewers. Out of these submissions, we selected 5 contributions as full papers yielding an acceptance rate of 29%. Further, we accepted two short papers representing promising research directions to spark discussions between researchers and practitioners on promising work in progress. This year, we have two scientific keynote speakers for the scientific program, who contribute two invited papers.

Main topics from academia and industry focused on Systems and Software Quality Management Methods, Improvements of Software Development Methods and Processes, latest trends and emerging topics in Software Quality, and Testing and Software Quality Assurance.

This book is structured according to the sessions of the scientific program following the guiding conference topic "Quality Intelligence in Software and Systems Engineering":

- Industry Challenges and Collaborations
- Software Testing Approaches
- Social Aspects in Software Engineering
- Natural Language Processing
- Software Quality Assurance Concepts

January 2020

Stefan Biffl
Dietmar Winkler
Daniel Mendez

Organization

SWQD 2020 was organized by Software Quality Lab GmbH, the Vienna University of Technology, Institute of Information Systems Engineering, and Blekinge Institute of Technology, Sweden.

Organizing Committee

General Chair

Johannes Bergsmann   Software Quality Lab GmbH, Austria

Scientific Program Co-chair

Stefan Biffl   TU Wien, Austria
Dietmar Winkler   TU Wien, Austria
Daniel Mendez   Blekinge Institute of Technology, Sweden

Proceedings Chair

Dietmar Winkler   TU Wien, Austria

Organizing and Publicity Chair

Petra Bergsmann   Software Quality Lab GmbH, Austria

Program Committee

SWQD 2020 established an international committee of well-known experts in software quality and process improvement to peer-review the scientific submissions.

Maria Teresa Baldassarre	University of Bari, Italy
Matthias Book	University of Iceland, Iceland
Ruth Breu	University of Innsbruck, Austria
Maya Daneva	University of Twente, The Netherlands
Oscar Dieste	Universidad Politécnica de Madrid, Spain
Andreas Ekelhart	SBA Research, Austria
Frank Elberzhager	Fraunhofer IESE, Germany
Michael Felderer	University of Innsbruck, Austria
Gordon Fraser	University of Passau, Germany
Nauman Ghazi	Blekinge Institute of Technology, Sweden
Volker Gruhn	University of Duisburg-Essen, Germany
Roman Haas	CQSE GmbH, Munich, Germany
Jens Heidrich	Fraunhofer IESE, Germany
Frank Houdek	Daimler AG, Germany
Marcos Kalinowski	Pontifical Catholic University of Rio de Janeiro, Brazil

Peter Kieseberg	FH St. Pölten, Austria
Eda Marchetti	ISTI-CNR, Italy
Kristof Meixner	TU Wien, Austria
Emilia Mendes	Blekinge Institute of Technology, Sweden
Paula Monteiro	CCG-Centro de Computação Gráfica, Portugal
Jürgen Münch	University of Reutlingen, Germany
Oscar Pastor	Universitat Politècnica de València, Spain
Dietmar Pfahl	University of Tartu, Estonia
Rick Rabiser	Johannes Kepler University Linz, Austria
Rudolf Ramler	Software Competence Center Hagenberg, Austria
Andreas Rausch	Technical University Clausthal, Germany
Felix Rinker	TU Wien, Austria
Klaus Schmid	University of Hildesheim, Germany
Miroslaw Staron	University of Gothenburg Gothenburg, Sweden
Andreas Vogelsang	Technische Universität Berlin, Germany
Rini Van Solingen	Delft University of Technology, The Netherlands
Henning Femmer	Qualicen GmbH, Germany
Kristian Beckers	Siemens AG, Germany
Sebastian Voss	fortiss GmbH, Germany
Stefan Wagner	University of Stuttgart, Germany

Additional Reviewers

Michael Brunner
Stefan Fischer
Andrea Mussmann

Contents

Industry Challenges and Collaborations

Together We Are Stronger: Evidence-Based Reflections on Industry-Academia Collaboration in Software Testing

Michael Felderer[1($\boxtimes$)] and Vahid Garousi[2]

[1] University of Innsbruck, Innsbruck, Austria
michael.felderer@uibk.ac.at
[2] Queen's University Belfast, Belfast, UK
v.garousi@qub.ac.uk

Abstract. For a highly relevant and applied research area like software testing industry-academia collaboration is of uttermost importance. In this paper we reflect on how industry-academia collaboration can be improved based on evidence from four empirical studies. We therefore first present four studies providing evidence on the (1) perceived level of challenges in testing activities, (2) focus areas in industrial and academic software testing conferences, (3) synergies between industrial and academic software testing conferences, as well as (4) the need for consideration of grey literature. Then, we reflect on issues, which we think can improve the link and synergies between industry and academia in software testing, i.e., research topics, guidelines and evidence, value and risk, context and scalability, action research and education as well as grey literature and open science.

Keywords: Software testing · Software quality · Industry academia collaboration

1 Introduction

In an applied research area like software engineering industrial impact and relevance are crucial [1]. This holds especially for software testing, which is an area of high scientific and practical importance as it comprises a critical set of activities to enable the development of high-quality software and systems [2].

This paper provides reflections on industry-academia collaboration in software testing, which aim to improve collaboration and as a follow-up impact of research in specific contexts and its transfer to practice. For that purpose, we first present studies providing evidence on industry-academia collaboration especially in software testing, but also its conferences and literature. We think that a holistic strategy to improving industry-academia collaboration requires to not

© Springer Nature Switzerland AG 2020
D. Winkler et al. (Eds.): SWQD 2020, LNBIP 371, pp. 3–12, 2020.
https://doi.org/10.1007/978-3-030-35510-4_1

only consider research topics, but also the research ecosystem, which includes conferences and literature, but also education.

This paper is structured as follows. Section 2 provides an overview of test activities. Section 3 provides available specific evidence on industry-academia collaboration in software testing as well as in its conferences and literature. Section 4 presents reflections on industry-academia collaboration based on the provided evidence. Finally, Sect. 5 concludes the paper.

2   Software Test Activities

According to the international testing standard ISO/IEC/IEEE 29119 [3], software testing comprises a set of activities conducted to facilitate discovery and/or evaluation of properties of one or more test items, i.e., a software system or parts of it. Following [4] we consider the nine test activities test-case design (criteria-based), test-case design (based on human expertise), test scripting, test execution, test evaluation, test-result reporting, test management, test automation, and other test activities. These test activities are defined in Table 1.

Table 1. Definition of test activity types [4]

Activity type	Description
Test-case design (criteria-based)	Designing test suites (set of test cases) or test requirements to satisfy coverage criteria, e.g., line coverage
Test-case design (based on human expertise)	Designing test suites (set of test cases) based on human expertise (e.g., exploratory testing) or other engineering goals
Test scripting	Documenting test cases in manual test scripts or automated test code
Test execution	Running test cases on the system under test (SUT) and recording the results
Test evaluation	Evaluating results of testing like assigning test verdicts
Test-result reporting	Reporting test verdicts and defects to developers, e.g., via defect (bug) tracking systems
Test management	Encompasses activities related to test management, e.g., planning, control, monitoring, etc.
Test automation	Automating any test activity
Other testing activities	Includes activities other than those discussed above, e.g., regression testing or test prioritization

3   Evidence on Industry-Academia Collaboration in Software Testing as Well as in Its Conferences and Literature

Software testing is an important area when investigating industry-academia collaboration in software engineering as it is a common topic covered in papers on industry-academia collaboration in software engineering in general as shown by a recent systematic literature review [5]. However, there are only a few studies focusing on industry-academia collaboration in software testing and providing evidence in that area. In this section we present four studies providing evidence on the perceived level of challenges in testing activities (Study 1), focus areas in industrial and academic software testing conferences (Study 2), synergies between industrial and academic software testing conferences (Study 3), as well as the need for consideration of grey literature (Study 4).

3.1   Study 1: Perceived Level of Challenges in Testing Activities

Garousi et al. [4] performed a survey among experienced practitioners to find out what industry wants from academia in software testing. For that purpose, practitioners were asked for the perceived level of challenges in testing activities as well as concrete research topics related to testing activities (see Table 1).

Figure 1 shows the level of challenges in each of the nine testing activities as perceived by the 105 participants of the survey.

Only for the activities of test management, test automation and other testing activities a significant amount of challenges is perceived by the participants. For these three activities, for instance the following concrete practically relevant topics, where solutions from research are required, are mentioned:

- *Test management*: test ROI calculation; risk metrics; test size and effort estimation; balance between test efficiency and effectiveness
- *Test automation*: metrics for test automation; fully-automated test script generation; usability of test automation; automated recommendation support for test execution
- *Other activities*: regression testing of complex legacy software; adoption of open source tools; test training and awareness.

3.2   Study 2: Focus Areas in Industrial and Academic Software Testing Conferences

Garousi and Felderer [6] compared presentation titles from several leading industrial and academic conferences. The top three terms were "automation", "mobile", and "agile" in industrial presentation titles and "model", "combinatorial", and "automated" in academic presentation titles, respectively. Both communities appear to focus on test automation. However, the presentation titles reveal that when practitioners refer to test automation, they mostly mean

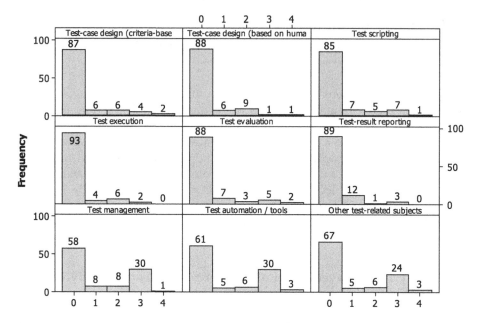

Fig. 1. Level of challenges in each testing activity (0 = no challenges at all, ..., 4 = lots of challenges) [4]

automating test execution. In contrast, academics focus mostly on automating other activities like test-case design or evaluation. Further industrial focus areas are test management and other activities like domain-specific aspects (e.g., mobile, robotics or cloud testing) as well as non-functional aspects like performance testing. This finding is inline with the industrial challenges raised in Fig. 1. Common presentation topics at academic conferences are search-based test-case design, combinatorial testing, mutation testing and model-based testing, i.e. topics at academic testing conferences seem to be mainly related to automated test-case design.

3.3 Study 3: Synergies Between Industrial and Academic Software Testing Conferences

Beszedes and Vidacs [7] compiled a comprehensive list of 63 academic and 38 industrial conferences that focus on testing aspects and analyzed their industry-academia synergies. For that purpose, they compute an index which considers chairs, presenters and keynotes from the other community (i.e., industry and academia, respectively) to measure synergies.

Figure 2 shows the presence of industrial chairs, PC members and keynote speakers in academic conferences and vice versa. Notable findings from this comparison are as follows:

– Academic conferences more often invite industrial members as program chairs than industrial conferences invite academic ones

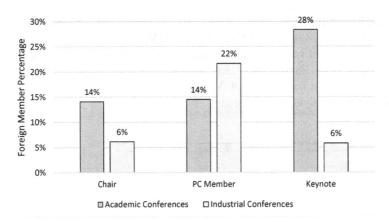

Fig. 2. Presence ratio of industrial members in academic conferences and vice versa) [7]

- Synergies regarding the membership of program committees are similar
- There are more keynotes with industrial background on academic conferences than academic keynotes on industrial ones
- Considering other factors as well, most notably the existence of a synergistic track, academic conferences show more ambitions to synergies
- In case of academic conferences, it seems that younger conferences are more industry oriented than the more mature ones.

Testing: Academia-Industry Collaboration, Practice and Research Techniques (TAIC PART) and Software Quality Days (SWQD) are rated and highlighted as distinguished venues to foster industry-academia collaboration in software testing and examples of mutual recognition between the two communities.

3.4 Study 4: Need for Consideration of Grey Literature

Garousi et al. [8] investigated the need for multivocal literature reviews in software engineering. Multivocal literature reviews [9] take grey literature into account in addition to formally published academic literature. Grey literature is typically neither formally peer-reviewed nor formally published, which implies uncertainty of the status of the covered information. Grey literature sources comprise for instance blog-like documents, videos, and white papers and are often written by practitioners to share their knowledge and opinions. The authors investigate, mainly based on examples from the domain of software testing, what types of knowledge are missed and what the software engineering community can gain when explicitly considering grey literature in literature studies.

For instance, Fig. 3, which is covered by the study, shows based on a multivocal literature review on test process assessment and improvement [10], what information from practice would have been missed if we were to exclude grey literature sources. Overall, 57 different test process assessment and improvement models were identified in the formal and grey literature sources of the performed multivocal literature review. From these sources 14 were grey literature reporting test maturity models such as TMap, Agile TMM or Test Maturity Index which would have been lost in a regular systematic literature review (by not including the grey literature). Furthermore, Fig. 3 shows the number of papers per model using or extending a source model. Without grey literature, the usage of TMap and some other models would not have been considered.

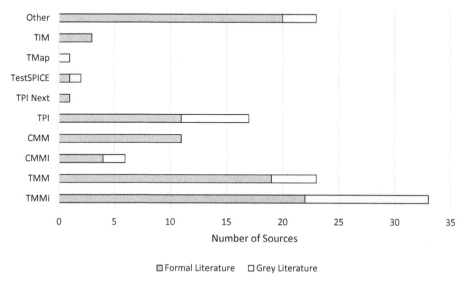

Fig. 3. Formal and grey literature per test process improvement model [10]

Based on a second multivocal literature review on test automation [11], also covered in the study by Garousi et al. [8], it is once more shown that a significant body of experience and knowledge from practicing test engineers on the topic of test automation would have been missed. To put this in quantitative terms, in the multivocal literature review factors to be considered for deciding when and what to automate in testing were analyzed by the type of source where they were mentioned. In total, 15 factor categories were identified, grey literature sources contributed a total of 219 occurrences of factors, while academic sources discussed only 67 occurrences. Furthermore, two factor categories (test oracle and development process) would not have been identified in the study if grey literature would not have been considered.

Based on these study, we can conclude that grey literature covers a large amount of knowledge, opinions and experience from practitioners and it can contribute substantially to the body of knowledge and open challenges in certain areas of software testing.

4 Reflections on Industry-Academia Collaboration in Software Testing

Based on the results of the studies and our own experiences we reflect on some issues that we consider relevant to benefit from industry-academia collaboration, especially in software testing, and to further improve the link and synergies between industry and academia.

Research Topics. Researchers should be aware of their industrial partners' challenges and take into account research topics that are novel, feasible, industrially relevant, and potentially impactful [12]. As highlighted in [4], problems, where practitioners require support from research, are especially related to test management and test automation. Garousi and Herkiloğlu [13] even propose a process to select suitable topics for industry-academia collaborations in software testing.

Guidelines and Evidence. Researchers can benefit a lot from available guidelines (e.g., technology transfer models [14] or patterns and anti-patterns [5]) and evidence on industry-academia collaboration in software engineering [15]. For instance, the first author of this paper was inspired by an available technology transfer model [14] when planning and performing research on testing with defect taxonomies in close collaboration with industry [16].

Value and Risk. Companies are under continuous pressure to make profit. Hence, researchers should take the business value into account and consider ideas from value-based software engineering [17]. Related to the concept of value is the concept of risk [18], which can be considered in all test activities [19]. For instance, risk (and therefore also value aspects) can be considered in test generation and selection approaches, which allows a much better business framing even of sophisticated test-generation approaches.

Context and Scalability. Software testing research has to become more context-driven by focusing on problems driven by concrete needs in specific domains and development projects. The applicability and scalability, which are essential for industrial acceptance and adoption of research results, depend largely on contextual factors, whether human (such as engineers' background), organizational (such as cost and time constraints), or domain-related (such as the level of criticality and compliance with standards) [20]. This also requires that top-journals and conferences acknowledge that context-driven research is needed, valuable, and challenging. Such research focuses especially on scalability in realistic conditions, and therefore brings essential contributions for an applied research field like software testing.

Action Research and Education. Action research [21], which seeks transformative change through the simultaneous process of taking action and doing research, is especially useful when collaborating with industry. It supports that the research problems are based on real industry needs and that research results are actually adopted in testing practice. Action research is often linked to education of practitioners. Especially software testing is considered as highly important, but with a considerable knowledge gap existing [22].

Grey Literature and Open Science. The dissemination of results, i.e., papers, artifacts and data, plays an important role in industry-academia collaboration. In addition, to research papers, researchers could try describing their research in laymen's terms, making it available in more forms than conference articles and journal papers. Knowledge should be made available through various forms of grey literature, e.g., by publishing slides, white papers, recorded videos, and blogs. On the other, hand researchers should also consider grey literature sources from practitioners as valuable sources to identify challenges, cases or even evidence. Researchers should also apply principles of open science [23], whose aim is to render all artifacts borne out of scientific research activities accessible, without any barriers, to any individual on Earth.

However, one should for sure also take into account that it is not achievable and even not desirable that industry and academia always collaborate very tightly. Wohlin [24] addresses this issues by defining five levels of closeness between industry and academia, i.e., not in touch, hearsay, sales pitch, offline, and one team. One should be aware that industry has for obvious reasons shorter cycle times, which implies moving targets and may pose impediments for long-term investigations and innovations researchers are aiming for. However, in an applied research area such as software testing, there should always be a link between industry and academia, which may vary in its intesnity. We hope that the raised issues support to keep continuously keep this link.

5   Conclusion

In this paper we first presented four studies providing evidence on the perceived level of challenges in testing activities (Study 1), focus areas in industrial and academic software testing conferences (Study 2), synergies between industrial and academic software testing conferences (Study 3), as well as the need for consideration of grey literature (Study 4). We then reflect on the following issues, which we think can improve the link and synergies between industry and academia in software testing: research topics, guidelines and evidence, value and risk, context and scalability, action research and education as well as grey literature and open science. Through papers such as this one, we're continuing our effort to bring practitioners and researchers in software testing closer to each other so that they can benefit each other much more than they do today.

Acknowledgments. The authors thank all collaborators from industry and academia who worked with them on industry-academia collaboration.

References

1. Lo, D., Nagappan, N., Zimmermann, T.: How practitioners perceive the relevance of software engineering research. In: Proceedings of the 2015 10th Joint Meeting on Foundations of Software Engineering, pp. 415–425. ACM (2015)
2. Harrold, M.J.: Testing: a roadmap. In: Proceedings of the Conference on the Future of Software Engineering, pp. 61–72. Citeseer (2000)
3. ISO: 29119-1-2013 - ISO/IEC/IEEE international standard - software and systems engineering -software testing -part 1: concepts and definitions (2013)
4. Garousi, V., Felderer, M., Kuhrmann, M., Herkiloğlu, K.: What industry wants from academia in software testing?: Hearing practitioners' opinions. In: Proceedings of the 21st International Conference on Evaluation and Assessment in Software Engineering, pp. 65–69. ACM (2017)
5. Garousi, V., Petersen, K., Ozkan, B.: Challenges and best practices in industry-academia collaborations in software engineering: a systematic literature review. Inf. Softw. Technol. **79**, 106–127 (2016)
6. Garousi, V., Felderer, M.: Worlds apart: industrial and academic focus areas in software testing. IEEE Softw. **34**(5), 38–45 (2017)
7. Beszédes, Á., Vidács, L.: Academic and industrial software testing conferences: survey and synergies. In: 2016 IEEE Ninth International Conference on Software Testing, Verification and Validation Workshops (ICSTW), pp. 240–249. IEEE (2016)
8. Garousi, V., Felderer, M., Mäntylä, M.V.: The need for multivocal literature reviews in software engineering: complementing systematic literature reviews with grey literature. In: Proceedings of the 20th International Conference on Evaluation and Assessment in Software Engineering, p. 26. ACM (2016)
9. Garousi, V., Felderer, M., Mäntylä, M.V.: Guidelines for including grey literature and conducting multivocal literature reviews in software engineering. Inf. Softw. Technol. **106**, 101–121 (2019)
10. Garousi, V., Felderer, M., Hacaloğlu, T.: Software test maturity assessment and test process improvement: a multivocal literature review. Inf. Softw. Technol. **85**, 16–42 (2017)
11. Garousi, V., Mäntylä, M.V.: When and what to automate in software testing? A multi-vocal literature review. Inf. Softw. Technol. **76**, 92–117 (2016)
12. Begel, A., Zimmermann, T.: Analyze this! 145 questions for data scientists in software engineering. In: Proceedings of the 36th International Conference on Software Engineering, pp. 12–23. ACM (2014)
13. Garousi, V., Herkiloglu, K.: Selecting the right topics for industry-academia collaborations in software testing: an experience report. In: 2016 IEEE International Conference on Software Testing, Verification and Validation (ICST), pp. 213–222. IEEE (2016)
14. Gorschek, T., Garre, P., Larsson, S., Wohlin, C.: A model for technology transfer in practice. IEEE Softw. **23**(6), 88–95 (2006)
15. Garousi, V., et al.: Characterizing industry-academia collaborations in software engineering: evidence from 101 projects. Empir. Softw. Eng. **24**, 1–63 (2019)
16. Felderer, M., Beer, A.: Mutual knowledge transfer between industry and academia to improve testing with defect taxonomies. In: Software-Engineering and Management 2015 (2015)
17. Ramler, R., Biffl, S., Grünbacher, P.: Value-based management of software testing. In: Biffl, S., Aurum, A., Boehm, B., Erdogmus, H., Grünbacher, P. (eds.) Value-Based Software Engineering, pp. 225–244. Springer, Heidelberg (2006). https://doi.org/10.1007/3-540-29263-2_11

18. Felderer, M., Schieferdecker, I.: A taxonomy of risk-based testing. Int. J. Softw. Tools Technol. Transf. **16**(5), 559–568 (2014)
19. Felderer, M., Ramler, R.: Integrating risk-based testing in industrial test processes. Softw. Qual. J. **22**(3), 543–575 (2014)
20. Basili, V., Briand, L., Bianculli, D., Nejati, S., Pastore, F., Sabetzadeh, M.: Software engineering research and industry: a symbiotic relationship to foster impact. IEEE Softw. **35**(5), 44–49 (2018)
21. Santos, P.S.M.d., Travassos, G.H.: Action research use in software engineering: an initial survey. In: Proceedings of the 2009 3rd International Symposium on Empirical Software Engineering and Measurement, pp. 414–417. IEEE Computer Society (2009)
22. Garousi, V., Giray, G., Tüzün, E., Catal, C., Felderer, M.: Aligning software engineering education with industrial needs: a meta-analysis. J. Syst. Softw. **156**, 65–83 (2019)
23. Fernández, D.M., Graziotin, D., Wagner, S., Seibold, H.: Open science in software engineering. arXiv preprint arXiv:1904.06499 (2019)
24. Wohlin, C.: Software engineering research under the lamppost. In: ICSOFT. IS-11 (2013)

Challenges in Testing Big Data Systems

An Exploratory Survey

Monika Steidl$^{(\boxtimes)}$, Ruth Breu, and Benedikt Hupfauf

Department of Computer Science, University of Innsbruck, Technikerstraße 21a,
6020 Innsbruck, Austria
Monika.Steidl@student.uibk.ac.at,
{Ruth.Breu,Benedikt.Hupfauf}@uibk.ac.at

Abstract. An increasing number of companies incorporate Big Data in order to increase business value and gain competitive advantages. With this new paradigm, also testing methodologies need to be revised to suit the specific requirements of Big Data. This paper summarizes the outcome of an exploratory survey conducted in 2018 with seven participants from different industries (Healthcare, Technology). The issues can be divided into four categories: (1) limited resources and performance problems, (2) verifying test results, (3) finding an optimal test coverage, and (4) availability of test data.

Keywords: System test for Big Data · Data-intensive · Test challenges · Exploratory survey · Big Data testing

1 Introduction

In recent years, Big Data has become an important driver of success in business. A survey conducted among 330 public North American companies evaluated their technology management practices. On average, the companies that used Big Data were six percent more profitable and five percent more productive than their direct competitors [1]. Another survey obtained similar results, when interviewing 341 businesses about their profitability with respect to Big Data [2]. The study found that the businesses that used data-intensive software were 36% more likely to achieve a stronger revenue growth, as well as a higher operating efficiency [1].

Although Big Data has the potential to gain significant competitive advantages with data driven decision making, more than a few companies fail to use these data successfully. A recent survey among nearly 65 industry leading firms and Fortune 1000 companies analysed, how Big Data and AI accelerate business transformation. The study found that even though most of the companies were investing in Big Data and AI, 37.8% did not report measurable results. Moreover, 77.1% stated that the adoption of Big Data or AI initiatives posed challenges for their organisations [3].

In this paper, Big Data and data-intensive are used synonymously and follow the definition of Mauro, Greco and Grimaldi: "Big Data is the Information asset characterized by such a High Volume, Velocity and Variety [and Veracity] to require specific Technology and Analytical Methods for its transformation into Value." [4].

Testing data-intensive systems is more challenging due to the data set's characteristics, however, crucial to prevent most critical failures. For instance, executing tests with a large volume of data as well as high velocity is very resource intensive. Also, the lack of homogeneity and standardization of the data types, structures and sources makes it significantly harder to test those systems [5].

This paper puts the main focus on challenges related to system tests, which are defined in this paper as testing the system as a whole. System testing is often referred to as Black Box testing, because tests are executed without knowledge about the internals of the system, such as code structure. In addition to tests for functional requirements, such as the correct behaviour of the system and robustness, also tests for non-functional requirements are considered. Non-functional requirements include for instance the scalability of a system, or its performance [6]. If not clearly stated otherwise, the terms test and system test are used as synonyms.

The paper is structured as follows: first, the objective for this survey is outlined in more detail, followed by a concise description of the methodological approach and the participants. Next, the analysis method is introduced. The main part of the paper summarizes the results and analyses the most frequently mentioned challenges in Big Data testing. Afterwards, threats to validity, related work and potential future work are discussed. The concluding chapter interprets the results and concludes the paper.

2 Objective

There is some evidence that the well-established practices of system testing do not necessarily apply to Big Data applications. We strive to fill this gap and further the understanding of system tests specifically designed for Big Data applications. For this, we collect the most common challenges from practice and build a taxonomy. Our main research question is:

RQ: "Which problems can arise when testing data intensive systems?"

With our work, we hope to facilitate the planning as well as the execution of tests, and ultimately reduce the risks of Big Data initiatives.

3 Methodological Approach and Survey Design

In order to answer the research question, a qualitative approach was chosen to explore and provide an insight into challenges during testing data-intensive systems. The qualitative approach is a valuable analysis method to understand individual experiences by outlining the complexity and diversity of the observed environment. Moreover, a qualitative survey does not restrict answers to a predefined set of options, but allows individuals to report their experiences in detail [7]. The data was collected with the help of seven semi-structured interviews. This allowed to elicit the interviewees' personal experience regarding system tests for data-intensive systems thoroughly. In addition, the semi-structured approach of the interviews allowed to further address the interviewees' responses, and to ask clarification questions [8].

The questionnaire consisted of a short introduction, the main part, and follow-up questions. The introductory questions included, for instance, the participant's definition of the terms "system test" and "Big Data", as well as a concise description of the participant's work experience in this field. This allowed to ensure a mutual understanding and minimize the risk of misconceptions. The main part included questions about testing guidelines and criteria, to obtain a better understanding on how extensively and precisely testing was done in their company. The general question was formulated as follow:

"What challenges have you noticed during your work life when using system tests for data-intensive applications/Big Data applications?"

Most of the time of the interview was dedicated to this open question, to avoid bias and allow the participants to express their personal opinion. During this part, follow up questions and clarification questions were allowed to ensure a mutual understanding of the presented issues and to gather enough details. This main question was answered by all participants without further need for structural questions. Thus, those structural question such as data issues, how to decide when the optimal test coverage was reached, and regression tests were used as sub questions. The interviews were conducted between 22 May 2018 and 15 June 2018 with an average duration of 34 min.

4 Participants

The target group for this survey comprised experts in software development and testing, who had at least five years of work experience with data-intensive applications. All interviewees participated voluntarily in the study without financial compensation and provided enough time to comprehensively answer all the survey questions. In order to protect their personal rights and their companies' intellectual property, the participants are only referred to by an ID. The participants work for four different companies; participants B and M work for an Austrian company in the Healthcare industry, participants F and C work for a Swiss company in the Healthcare industry, participant L works for a US software company, and finally, participants I and A work for an Austrian company specializing in software testing. Although all participants are located in Europe, their companies operate world-wide. For further information on the field of work, years of work experience, industry, number of company employees and region, see Table 1.

Table 1. Description of the participants

ID	Field of work	Experience	Industry	#Employees	Region
B	ADF database	13 years	Healthcare	1.500	AT
F	AI/Machine learning	19 years	Healthcare	25.000	CH
C	BI	13 years	Healthcare	25.000	CH
L	Machine learning	8 years	Technology	10.000	NO
M	ERP-Systems	16 years	Healthcare	1.500	AT
I	AI/Machine learning	11 years	Technology	500	AT
A	BI/Data warehouse	10 years	Technology	500	AT

5   Analysis Method

The evaluation of the interviews was based on the summarizing qualitative content analysis described by Mayring [7]. This approach systematically reduces the amount of data collected in the interviews, while still maintaining a realistic depiction of the base material. We opted for an inductive category definition method [7] that is described in more detail in the course of this section. In order to gain a neutral and objective insight into the collected material, without having prepossessions based on a literature review prior to the analysis, we derived categories from the interviews without references to previously designed theory concepts.

Based on the inductive category definition by Mayring [7] for the first step, awareness was raised for the aim of the survey: Identifying problems regarding system tests for data intensive applications. In the second step, categories were defined. For the questions about the interviewee's definitions of the terms Big Data and system tests as well as his/her background, the following four categories were created: "work experience", "Big Data", "system tests" and "quality criteria". For the research related questions, the categories "data", "validation of sufficiency of number of tests", "regression tests" and "verification of results" were defined.

In the third step, statements were allocated to categories defined in step two, with the help of segmentation and subsumption. By the means of segmentation, we divided the content into units of coding, which are defined as short and content-focused paraphrases where extraneous details are omitted [7]. Those segments were then added to a category via subsumption [7, 9]. However, when the segment did not match any category, a new category was added. The following categories were added: "resources", "statistics and testing", "continuous ongoing system testing", "repeatability", "machine learning" and "performance". Additionally, although mentioned infrequently, the categories "human layer and automatization", "user acceptance testing" and "testing as a discipline" were added.

As an intermediate step, after assigning approximately half of the interview material to the categories, the material was revised to check if the analysis still fulfilled the purpose of the survey as defined in step one. Based on Mayring's approach [7] step two was also executed again to revise the segments in the category and relocate the segments if they fitted better to a newly created category. In addition, the abstraction level was also amended.

6   Results

This section presents the main findings of the survey. For a better understanding of the most common challenges in testing Big Data systems, the results are divided in four main categories: (1) limited resources and performance problems, (2) verifying test results, (3) finding an optimal test coverage, and (4) availability of test data. Each sub-section is dedicated to one of the aforementioned categories and begins with a summary of the most important statements of the participants. In addition, a table provides a summary of all statements related to this category, where columns represent topics, and rows represent participants. A checkmark indicates that the participant saw the topic in question as a challenge, whereas a cross indicates that the participant did not see this topic as a challenge. If neither a checkmark nor a cross is depicted, the participant did not mention the topic at all.

6.1   Resources and Performance

The interviewees B, F, L, M and I stated that resources played a significant role in their testing environment. One of the most frequently mentioned challenges were the **hardware, and storage capacity**. B and L stated that when testing the system with loads of collected real time data, a lot of processing cores were required. In addition, data that needed to be processed could not fit into the main memory. Participant F, L and I also stated that repeating and comparing tests caused storage issues, because for every test run, the version of the system as well as the input data set needed to be documented and archived. Moreover, participant I stated that he needed different data sets to execute the system test. Considering the number of tests done for each version and the according data used, led to a huge amount of data that needed to be stored. According to F, L, and I, this could lead to a high administrative burden regarding memory consumption and storage.

When talking about **costs**, B, M, and I stated that the hardware to run the tests was expensive. When using different environments for testing and production, replicating the live system one-to-one led to a significant increase in costs, and budget restrictions prohibited duplicating the production environment. In addition, the production environment might use thousands of machines located at various parts of the world, which would increase the complexity of the test environment significantly. They frequently had to deal with a trade-off between money and risk when testing – the higher the investment, the better the replication of the testing environment, the more extensive and realistic tests could be executed.

When there were limited resources, **performance** was directly affected. This challenge was mentioned by the participants M and I, while participant A denied that performance was a challenge when directly asked about it. The reason why participant A never encountered performance deviation between test and production environments was that he integrated software into an already existing system landscape and focused more on functional requirements than performance. Nevertheless, participant M stated that the performance in the testing environment was worse than in the production environment due to limited resources available or different network dependencies. Participant M stated that they encountered a problem with the utilization of I/O interfaces, because they were busy with backups at night. Consequently, the performance of a newly implemented software under test deteriorated substantially. Furthermore, according to participants M and I, it was challenging to derive performance measures from just testing the system with a small data set. Consequently, such a test would not be suitable to predict the software's behaviour beforehand.

Contrary to participant M, participant I stated that his company did not measure performance in the test environment due to the lack of expressivity. Consequently, they had to monitor performance directly in the production environment. On the downside, the current workload of the system had a major influence on the system's performance and could not be predicted easily beforehand. A summary of the most important statements with respect to this category, Resources and Performance, can be found in Table 2.

Table 2. Overview of the statements related to the category Resources and Performance

ID	Hardware & storage capacity	Budget & money	Performance
B	✓ Require processing cores	✓ Budget restrictions	
F	✓ Storing test data		
C			
L	✓ Saving and processing data		
M		✓ Trade-off between money and risk	✓ Limited resources cause unforeseeable problems
I	✓ Storing test data	✓ Replication of production environment	✓ Different workload in production and test
A			✗

6.2 Verifying Test Results

The challenge of verifying test results was never mentioned by the participants on their initiative. However, when asked directly, the majority of participants acknowledged that verifying test results was challenging. Interviewees M, I and A stated that they had fundamental problems to **define a test oracle**. The oracle was based on a design documentation, the acceptance criteria of user stories in the agile context, or the subjective opinion of the testers, which could impose some bias on the test results. In all cases, humans made the decision to define how reliable the test results were.

Participant F and I stated that when talking about test verification in the **machine learning context**, test cases were based on a statistical approach. Tests were done with data sets, where the output was already known and evaluated accordingly. However, they found it difficult to evaluate the output when new test data sets were used, or the algorithm changed its behaviour. Moreover, participant I stated that testing machine learning algorithms was particularly challenging, when the desired output was simply unknown (e.g. unsupervised learning). A summary of the most important statements with respect to this category, Verifying Test Results, can be found in Table 3.

Table 3. Overview of the statements related to the category Verifying Test Results

ID	Test oracle	Testing machine learning
B		
F		✓ Verify output of new test data set
C		
L		
M	✓ Validate results without human interaction	
I	✓ Based on subjective criteria	✓ Difficult to know which output is expected
A	✓ Define business tests	

6.3 Finding an Optimal Test Coverage

All participants stated that it was difficult to decide, when the **optimal test coverage** was reached for multiple reasons. For instance, participant I found it difficult to measure test coverage in general. Moreover, multiple participants saw a trade-off between high test coverage on the one hand, and budget, resources, or risk on the other.

Participants L, M, I and A had some **rules or guidelines** with respect to the test coverage required by their companies. For instance, participants I and A relied on risk assessment to find an optimal test coverage. Interviewee I used a tree like hierarchy to focus on the tests with the highest priority. He, as well as participant M, argued that finding an optimal test coverage was a general problem in testing, and not unique for testing Big Data applications. To tackle this problem, participant M introduced a "signature approach", where the person in charge had to sign that a sufficient test coverage had been reached. This way, managers were in charge of test coverage and had to take responsibility. According to participant A, to accurately assess the risk and make a thoughtful decision, requirement management needed to understand the complexity of the system, which was often challenging. Interviewee F and L chose a different approach and focused on the need of having a statistically representative number of test cases. For participant L, it was an issue which number of test cases was representative in order to ensure that the system functioned properly. Participant B remarked that he did not have any formal metrics for optimal test coverage and based his decisions on work experience and guess work.

Finally, one of participant B's challenges was the trade-off between time and system reliability, which was also mentioned by participant A. A summary of the most important statements with respect to this category, Finding an Optimal Test Coverage, can be found in Table 4.

Table 4. Overview of the statements related to the category Finding an Optimal Test Coverage

ID	Optimal test coverage	No rules	Time
B	✓	✓ No formal metrics (work experience & guess work)	✓ Trade-off between time & reliability
F	✓	✓ Statistically representative number of samples	
C	✓		
L	✓	✓ Statistically representative number of samples	
M	✓	✗ Signature approach to verify test coverage	
I	✓	✗ Risk based test tree structure	
A	✓	✓ Understand system requirements	✓ Time and resources

6.4 Availability of Test Data

The **absence of data** was mentioned by all participants. The answers included technical, as well as organizational issues. Participant B stated that data was sparsely available.

This challenge was particularly problematic with data from the healthcare sector or the government, due to strict privacy guidelines. According to interviewee L, unavailable servers or broken sensors, which were not sending information anymore, contributed to the problem of missing data. Another reason for missing data mentioned by participant I was that historical data was not available for newly implemented functions. Additionally, interviewee M gave prominence to data availability problems because of a lack of communication between different departments. In essence, the departments simply did not know which data was already available. However, also internal access restrictions could apply, as in the case of interviewee I. When applying for test data, it took up to several weeks until the data set was allocated. Subsequently, the testing process was prolonged due to temporarily unavailable data. Participants B and C also stated that full data integrity was exceedingly difficult to achieve. It was impossible to have all the data available everywhere simultaneously. Moreover, participant F took into consideration that his company was not willing to use production data for testing purposes. Notwithstanding, production data was absolutely necessary to ensure well-conducted system tests. Moreover, when talking about production data used for system tests, participant I raised concerns that data which was not created synthetically, was getting depleted too quickly under the assumption that several system tests were executed per day. Thus, when testing, the company could run out of data to use.

Another challenge in this category were **data protection regulations**. This challenge was indicated by most of the participants, in particular by participant F. He was working in the healthcare sector where he would have needed patient records for testing. However, regulations prohibited him from using raw data. Even anonymizing the test data did not fulfil the strict data protection rules of his company, because the risk of deanonymization and violating privacy regulations was too high. This is even more true since the new General Data Protection Regulations (GDPR). For instance, the companies of participants I and M needed to be more careful when processing data and implement anonymization strategies. With respect to anonymization, participant M highlighted that the characteristics of the data needed to be preserved.

In contrast, participants C and A did not face any challenges with respect to test data because of data protection regulations. Interviewee C only used internal and process specific data that were not protected by any regulations. Participant A, on the other hand, stated that they very rarely used data from production; however, when they used it, the data sets were anonymized and masked. Furthermore, he used synthetical data that was generated, which also did not pose any data regulation problems.

Another challenge identified in the course of the interviews were problems related to the **different structure, formats, and sources** of data, all of which are characteristics associated with Big Data. Participant B worked in a project for processing natural language and they were severely struggling with different formats and sources. Participant L and A emphasized the difficulty of integrating data into one universal format. In addition, data was messy, unstructured, full of errors, excessively big and constantly changing. Due to these characteristics of Big Data, interviewee L also struggled to verify if there were no duplicates included and if the data was consistent. When it came to the successful usage of data in system tests, participants M, I, and A also needed to have the data in a harmonized and purified way, stored somewhere accessible. Interviewee I conducted a survey where they found that due to insufficient data preparations in their company, 32% of all automated test cases failed. To fix the failing tests, maintenance costs and processing time increased.

Another challenge mentioned by participants F, C, L, M, I and A was the trade-off between the **size of the data set and representability**. Participant C and F stated, that a frequent question in their company was, how much data was needed to properly model the relation and behaviour patterns of the data set used in production. A test data set might be correct in the structural and relational perspective, but not representative, because the statistical behaviour was different than the one in the complete data set.

Furthermore, participant M touched upon the appropriate size of the test data set. Normally, systems were tested with a small data set, although Big Data needed to be processed when the system is used in production. The data-intensive software's load was created by processing the data. Therefore, performance could not sufficiently be tested with a small data set.

Participant C and A also emphasized that the composition of the data set was a much-discussed topic and needed a lot of time to search for the right data, so that data scientists as well as people from the business side felt comfortable. Additionally, understanding the business relations between data was essential to finding the right data set for testing.

When production data was not an option, participants C, L and I relied on **data generators**, although generating synthetical data was costly and posed a substantial effort. They claimed that synthetic data sets did not reflect the intended behaviour between objects. According to interviewee F and M, the synthetical data set could be biased, depending on how the data generation algorithm was implemented. The algorithm was based on a finite set of criteria which the business side and software deployment team determined. Participant I elaborated that in his case only 80 to 85% of the automated test cases worked properly with synthetically produced data. Those data worked perfectly until the test case required historical data, which caused the test case to collapse.

In contrast to the others, participants L and M saw the decision of which data set to use not as part of the system test, but as part of the architectural phase. Since the technical and business side needed to agree on what was the purpose of the system and which data needed to be collected in the beginning, interviewee L and M saw the collection of data sets more as preparatory work. Nonetheless, participant M and L confirmed that defining test data sets was an arduous task and the mentioned problems beforehand were applicable. A summary of the most important statements with respect to this category, Availability of Test Data, can be found in Table 5.

Table 5. Overview of the statements related to the category Availability of Test Data

ID	Availability	Data protection regulation	Structure, format, sources	Size of data set	Data generator
B	✓ Private database		✓ Jungle of data		
F	✓ Not using production data	✓ Healthcare sector		✓ Model behaviour pattern	✓ Biased
C	✓ Data integrity	✗ Internal, product specific data	✓ Data preparation	✓ Model behaviour pattern	✓ Instead of pseudonymisation
L	✓ Unavailable servers (preparatory work)	✓ User data	✓ Purify data	✓	✓
M	✓ Unawareness of data (preparatory work)	✓ Obfuscation	✓ Purify data	✓ Performance	✓ Deviations
I	✓ No historic data	✓ Transaction histories	✓ Data preparation	✓	✓ Prone to errors
A	✓ Unaware	✗ Internal data	✓ Purify data	✓	

7 Threats to Validity

The guidelines elaborated by Cook and Campbell [10] form the basis for further argumentations. Concerning external validity, a two-stage selection process was applied to ensure a better generalization possibility. We defined a target group as described in the section Participants and chose a random sample of the target group. This helped minimizing the threat of a too biased selection of interview partners. However, the sampling number comprised only seven people working in a similar region, which limits the insights into diverse cultural mindsets and companies' system testing cultures; however, all companies are operating internationally. It remains open whether the results can be generalized to other geographical regions, which could be subject to further research.

Additionally, half of the samples were taken from companies in the healthcare sector with stricter guidelines compared to other companies [11]. Thus, the findings may not apply to companies working in different sectors. However, the healthcare and technology sectors are precursors of Big Data Applications, undergoing rapid transformation to keep up to date with software requirements. Since quality and reliability are paramount in these sectors, one could argue that they are a good starting point to come to a deeper understanding of the challenges in testing Big Data systems.

Finally, the ranking of the challenges is not completely objective due to the small sample size. Not all challenges were covered in detail by every single participant because of the wide range of possible challenges and the participants' duty of confidentiality. However, the aim of this paper was not to find an absolute ranking of challenges in testing Big Data systems, but to gain an understanding of the challenges and build a taxonomy.

8 Related Work

Bertolino [12] investigated the challenges of conventional software testing in 2007. Bertolino identified several challenges, including test effectiveness, a test oracle, automating tests, test input generation, and costs. Although the research had no special focus on Big Data systems, we found that the challenges still applied to many of the participants of this survey. For instance, test input generation was still a major challenge for most participants. Even more so, as the characteristics of Big Data systems add another layer of complexity.

Tao et al. [13] compared the characteristics of conventional testing and Big Data application testing. As even a short summary of the comparison would go beyond the scope of this paper, the reader is referred to the original publication. In addition, they argue that there were increasing quality problems in the field of Big Data applications. For this, they too analyzed challenges related to quality assurance in Big Data systems. They conclude that finding an adequate test model, such as a test oracle, and test coverage are major issues. Both issues were also mentioned multiple times by the participants in this survey. Moreover, Tao et al. [13] identified the lack of quality assurance standards and test automation tools as issues. However, these issues were only mentioned infrequently by the participants of this survey. In addition, we identified several challenges not mentioned by Tao et al. These include the trade-off between time and test coverage, budgetary constraints and availability of test data.

Libes et al. [14] conducted a survey in the advanced manufacturing industry with focus on the availability of test data to highlight the challenges of system tests. Their main concern was real-life data availability, such as missing data types or an insufficient data quantity. They also touched upon access and usage preventions due to strict data protection regulations and data sets with missing values. In advanced manufacturing, data may also have been collected or generated with different underlying goals. Also a lack of documentation of the data formats make it hard to interpret and use the data sets [14]. A different study, conducted by Kanstren [15], also mentioned data absence in his experience report of testing data-intensive systems. Access restrictions and limited visibility within the company inhibited using the available data as test data [15]. Both papers are limited to challenges related to the availability of test data. Although the availability of test data was frequently mentioned during the interviews, we found that testers faced a wider range of challenges in practice.

Alexandrov et al. [16] analyzed the challenges of testing Big Data applications. However, they only researched the generation of test data.

9 Future Work

In future research, the findings of this survey could be verified at a larger scale. A bigger number of participants and a broader field of companies (geographic location, sector) help to further strengthen the results presented.

The findings of this paper give rise to several areas for further research. The problems of the category **Resources and performance** mostly stem from the idea that the test environment should be as close to the production environment as possible. Future research could look into possible ways of scaling down the test environment or data sets while maintaining their characteristics (also see [17]).

When it comes to **Verifying test results,** future work could investigate new oracles and metamorphic testing to overcome limitations when testing Big Data systems.

Finally, the challenges of the category **Availability of test data** could be addressed in future research by the means of anonymisation techniques and data generators.

10 Conclusion

The main objective of this paper was to address the lack of research for system tests for data-intensive applications. Originally, the research question was formulated as follows: **"Which problems can arise when testing data-intensive systems?"**. An exploratory survey with seven interview partners was conducted in order to further the understanding of common challenges in testing Big Data systems. We identified numerous challenges and grouped them in four main categories: (1) limited resources and performance problems, (2) verifying test results, (3) finding an optimal test coverage, and (4) availability of test data.

The first category, limited resources, and performance problems included challenges related to the high demand of computation power, memory, and storage capacity. Moreover, high costs and the fact that it is hard to estimate the performance of a system based on a non-production environment were mentioned frequently.

The challenges grouped in the second category, verifying test results, included defining test cases, validating test results without human interaction, and specifying the desired output for test cases. The latter was challenging in particular in a machine learning context, where the desired output is simply unknown (e.g. when applying unsupervised learning).

The third category, finding an optimal test coverage, was characterized by a trade-off between high test coverage on the one hand, and money, time, and resources on the other hand. In addition, many participants found the lack of clear guidelines on test coverage in their company challenging.

The last category, availability of test data, was the most comprehensive category. The participants mentioned an extensive list of reasons why test data was not available: regulations, policies, private databases, a lack of communication between different departments, or non-existent historic data for new functions. Furthermore, key characteristics of Big Data turned out to be challenging for system tests. For instance, the high volume of data posed a major challenge. The same holds for unstructured data, diverse formats, and different sources (variety). In order to compensate for the lack of test data, many companies used data generators. However, synthetic data posed a challenge in itself for most participants.

We found that the last category, availability of test data, was the most frequently mentioned category. All participants saw at least two of the five topics as a challenge. Thus, we conclude that the quality of test data is among the most critical factors for successful and expressive system tests for data-intensive applications.

References

1. McAfee, A., Brynjolfsson, E.: Big Data: the management revolution. Harv. Bus. Rev. **90**, 60-6, 68, 128 (2012)
2. Marshall, A., Mueck, S., Shockley, R.: How leading organizations use Big Data and analytics to innovate. Strategy Leadersh. **43**, 32–39 (2015)
3. NewVantage Partners LLC: Big Data and AI Executive Survey 2019: Data and Innovation How Big Data and AI are Accelerating Business Transformation (2019). Accessed 30 May 2019 https://newvantage.com/wp-content/uploads/2018/12/Big-Data-Executive-Survey-2019-Findings-Updated-010219-1.pdf
4. De Mauro, A., Greco, M., Grimaldi, M.: A formal definition of Big Data based on its essential features. Libr. Rev. **65**, 122–135 (2016)
5. Myers, G.J., Sandler, C., Badgett, T.: The Art of Software Testing. Wiley, Hoboken (2012)
6. Ammann, P., Offutt, J.: Introduction to Software Testing. Cambridge University Press, Cambridge (2008)
7. Mayring, P.: Qualitative Inhaltsanalyse: Grundlagen und Techniken. Beltz, Weinheim (2010)
8. Creswell, J.W.: Research Design: Qualitative, Quantitative, and Mixed Methods Approaches. SAGE Publ., Los Angeles (2010)
9. Schreier, M.: Qualitative Content Analysis in Practice. SAGE, Los Angeles, London, New Delhi, Singapore, Washington DC (2012)
10. Cook, T.D., Campbell, D.T.: Quasi-Experimentation: Design & Analysis Issues for Field Settings. Houghton Mifflin, Boston (1979)
11. IMDRF SaMD Working Group: Software as a Medical Device (SaMD): Application of Quality Management System (2015). http://www.imdrf.org/workitems/wi-samd.asp. Accessed 21 July 2018
12. Bertolino, A.: Software testing research: achievements, challenges, dreams. In: Briand, L.C., Wolf, A.L. (eds.) Future of Software Engineering, 2007: FOSE 2007, 29th International Conference on Software Engineering, ICSE 2007, Minneapolis, Minnesota, 23–25 May 2007, pp. 85–103. IEEE Computer Society, Los Alamitos (2007)
13. Tao, C., Gao, J.: Quality assurance for Big Data application – issuses, challenges, and needs. In: Proceedings of the 28th International Conference on Software Engineering and Knowledge Engineering, pp. 375–381. KSI Research Inc. and Knowledge Systems Institute Graduate School (2016)

14. Libes, D., Lechevalier, D., Jain, S.L.: Issues in synthetic data generation for advanced manufacturing. In: Nie, J.-Y. (ed.) 2017 IEEE International Conference on Big Data: Proceedings, Boston, MA, USA, 11–14 December 2017, pp. 1746–1754. IEEE, Piscataway (2017)
15. Kanstren, T.: Experiences in testing and analysing data intensive systems. In: Proceedings of the 2017 IEEE International Conference on Software Quality, Reliability and Security (Companion Volume): QRS-C 2017, IEEE International Conference on Software Quality RaS, Prague, Czech Republic, 25–29 July 2017, pp. 589–590. IEEE, Piscataway (2017)
16. Alexandrov, A., Brücke, C., Markl, V.: Issues in Big Data testing and benchmarking. In: Narasayya, V., Polyzotis, N., Ailamaki, N. (eds.) DBTest 2013: Proceedings of the Sixth International Workshop on Testing Database Systems, New York, NY, USA, p. 1. Association for Computing Machinery, New York (2013)
17. Madhavji, N.H., Miranskyy, A., Kontogiannis, K.: Big picture of Big Data software engineering: with example research challenges. In: Proceedings of the First International Workshop on Big Data Software Engineering - BIGDSE 2015, Florence, Italy, 23 May 2015, pp. 11–14. IEEE, Piscataway (2015)

Software Testing Approaches

Selecting and Prioritizing Regression Test Suites by Production Usage Risk in Time-Constrained Environments

Daniel Lübke[(✉)][iD]

FG Software Engineering, Leibniz Universität Hannover, Hannover, Germany
daniel.luebke@inf.uni-hannover.de

Abstract. Regression Testing is an important quality assurance activity for combating unwanted side-effects, which might have been introduced in a new software release. Selecting and prioritizing regression test cases is a challenge in practice – especially in a world of ever increasing complexity, distribution, and size of the software solutions. Current approaches try to minimize the number of regression test cases by analyzing the change and the coverage of the tests with regards to this change. Our approach utilizes usage frequencies from the previous, productive software version in order to select or prioritize test cases by calculating the Regression Risk of a change. This takes into account that not all features of a software are used the same. We successfully validate our approach in a case study of an industry project which develops a complex process integration platform.

Keywords: Regression test · Software test · Risk · Test coverage · Test priorization · Test selection · Regression Risk Coverage

1 Introduction

Testing is the execution of a software system with the goal to find errors [30]. "[It] is an essential activity in software engineering" [4] and is probably the most important quality assurance technique employed in today's software projects, consuming half of the projects' budgets [12].

In practical terms testing can never be complete: "Because software and any digital systems are not continuous, testing boundary values are not sufficient to guarantee correctness. All the possible values need to be tested and verified, but complete testing is infeasible." [31] If we look at the complexity and the possible value space of even modest service designs alone, the value space and its combinations are far too large to even try to cover all values. For example, the SOAP-based eBay API[1] contains 8199 different XML elements.

Thus, testing cannot be complete and cannot demonstrate the absence of defects. However, the more tests have been performed, the more defects are

---

[1] https://developer.ebay.com/webservices/latest/ebaySvc.wsdl.

© Springer Nature Switzerland AG 2020
D. Winkler et al. (Eds.): SWQD 2020, LNBIP 371, pp. 31–50, 2020.
https://doi.org/10.1007/978-3-030-35510-4_3

found but the higher the costs. Therefore, testing can be seen as a risk mitigation technique.

As with any risk management activity, the intensity of testing is also a commercial question. The more tests are being performed, the higher the costs. While the costs usually increase at least linearly, the number of found defects decreases exponentially. Thus, the goal in most commercial software projects is to find a optimal trade-off between testing activities and the remaining risk in terms of undetected defects delivered into production.

One important type of tests are regression tests. Regression tests are "performed on modified software to provide confidence that changes are correct and do not adversely affect other portions of the software" [36]. Ideally, regression tests enable a smooth transition of a new version of a software system into production without unnoticed "side-effects", i.e., defects.

With the rise of more complex software systems, e.g., large cloud-enabled systems based on a microservice architecture, which are based on a multitude of services, regression test suites need to increase in size in order to find critical defects prior to release. Test generation approaches, e.g., Combinatorial Test Design (CTD) [6,9] can be used for generating large test suites with high code coverage. While more faults can be detected with such test suites, these test suites require extensive time to run. Usually, today's complex systems cannot be tested overnight anymore: "Re-running all existing test cases is often costly and sometimes even infeasible due to time and resource constraints." [2]. In the case study project Terravis [28] automated end-to-end process unit tests take around 4 s, automated integration tests 1.5 min, and automated system-level tests take approx. 5 min per end-to-end process variant. This means that only 96 end-to-end process tests on system level can be executed in 8 h, if no parallelization occurs. Such projects tend to implement complex executable business processes [13] with even more complex data-transformation logic [25]. Regression testing in such projects is very important because they have lots of code changes over time that requires frequent regression testing [19].

With the rise of DevOps practices, which include continuous builds and deployments, it is even more critical that a deployment is not blocked by tests but can instead go live quickly because otherwise the envisioned flexibility and deployment speed cannot be realized. Thus, testers of such complex systems need to find ways to reduce the time required for running regression tests. Marijan et al. have worked on how projects can "learn" to optimize testing in such scenarios [26].

First countermeasures can be non-algorithmic. By parallelizing test runs, the project must invest into development infrastructure but can reduce the time of regression tests easily. Another option is to cover more aspects in more technical tests. Because unit tests run much faster than system tests, as many aspects as possible should be covered there. However, unit tests are usually developed and maintained by the developers so that the different perspective of a tester is missing. Even more importantly, unit tests – by definition – cannot find integration issues, which need to be tested for in different tests.

By having smaller deployment units, e.g., in microservice architectures, the test scope is reduced even without applying any selection or prioritization techniques, because the system is composed of many, smaller sub-systems, which are strongly isolated.

However, moving more aspects to unit and integration tests and solely relying on the deployment unit scope pose the risk of missing defects that got introduced by integration problems. Because today's systems are often distributed, changes can leak via many channels; for instance via APIs and services (e.g., by broken backwards-compatibility in the service contract) or via Web pages (e.g., transclusion of another page might fail or a robot cannot handle the page anymore). Due to the increasing use of non-formal descriptions of services (e.g., most REST services are described on Web pages in a semi-structured way), static analysis for automatically determining the impact of the change is becoming increasingly harder. Also applications built with a microservice architecture tend to use even looser-coupled technologies like messaging and eventing, so that receivers are unknown to static inspection by design.

On the one hand, these developments make regression test selection and reduction techniques ever more important but on the other hand these techniques work only well within single deployment units or systems which are connected with formal service contracts. This is because current techniques mostly utilize knowledge that can be extracted from the system during design time (e.g., static analysis like control-flow graphs) and thus cannot be applied if at design time certain judgements cannot be made. For example, the control-flow graph of microservice architecture systems cannot be constructed anymore because service dependencies cannot be resolved at design-time without requiring further, usually unavailable, information.

Therefore, this paper proposes to complement existing techniques with an approach, which we call Regression Risk Coverage: The idea is to use dynamic data collected at run-time in order to select and/or prioritize regression tests. Most frequently used functionalities are deemed more critical and thus test cases covering those are selected first and/or with higher priority.

This paper is structured as follows: In the next Section related work is presented. Section 3 introduces the concepts Regression Risk and Regression Risk Coverage before an example is given in Sect. 4. Application of the newly proposed metrics are validated in a case study presented in Sect. 5. Finally, a conclusion and an outlook are given in Sect. 6.

2   Related Work

Regression testing has been a research topic for a long time. Rothermell and Herold [35] have compiled a list of the then available regression test techniques. The extensive description has been summarized by Kim and Porter [15] as they fitted the different algorithms to the following categories:

Retest-All Technique: This technique runs all available regression tests not considering any optimization possibilities, e.g., by analyzing the change in the software.

Random/Ad-Hoc Technique: Testers or an algorithm selects a random subset of regression tests or a subset based on their personal experience.

Minimization Technique: Such techniques try to select a minimal subset of the regression tests so that all changes in the software are covered.

Safe Technique: Such techniques identify all regression test cases that cover a change in the software system and select those for execution.

Later, Kim and Porter [15] present their approach, which takes more data as input. They model regression testing not as a single, one-time activity but as a sequence of test runs, which better reflects the activities in a software project. If testing finds a defect prior to release, it is generally fixed and re-tested. Thus, testing is indeed a sequence of different test runs. By taking into account what tests have been previously run and which test cases failed and which passed allows to make better judgements about which tests to select next. This is especially important in resource constrained environments, which are not capable of running all test cases in a single test run. For example, nightly builds are constrained in the time tests may run. It therefore makes no sense to re-run the same tests on the next day. Other tests can be chosen to cover more parts of the software with each additional nightly build.

Existing techniques have been refined since. For example, Panda and Mohapatra use integer linear programming models to minimize test suites [32].

A recent survey about test case priorization techniques has been compiled by Mukherjee and Patnaik [29]. Since the report of Rothermell and Herold additional techniques have been proposed. This especially includes techniques that utilize additional data sources. Further, history-based data, e.g., test case costs [33], test case success rate [16] and fault severity [33] are used as inputs for prioritizing test cases.

Wong et al. [39] showed that smaller test suites are as effective in finding defects as larger ones, if coverage is kept constant. Thereby, they concluded that a test suite can be minimized by removing all test cases, which do not increase the coverage over the already selected test case set.

Graves et al. have conducted experiments [11] for comparing different selection techniques. They found that the efficiency depends on the available test suite, the changes made to the software, and the characteristics of the software itself.

All such approaches are based on an existing test suite. If none exists, it needs to be created. Shihab et al. [38] have compiled a list of heuristics that can be used to develop unit tests to existing legacy code bases.

If a regression test suite detects a fault, the problem is how to diagnose its root cause. Selecting the matching test cases in order to help the diagnosis, Gonzales et al. have developed an approach to select test cases for this use case [10].

In a recent literature review, Mukherjee et al. [29] complied an extensive list of algorithms and empirical research regarding test case priorization to which the reader is referred to for further information.

Previous works have shown that using production data for guiding or helping software development projects can be useful; especially in the realm of testing.

For example, regression tests can be mined from process logs [20] in order to replicate defects on non-production machines and to have a test case that verifies the fix in all upcoming releases.

Therefore, we add an additional data source in this article, which is not exploited in previous works: the information about (user) behaviour in the productive system.

Felderer and Schieferdecker [8] give a taxonomy for risk-based testing. They identify risk drivers, risk assessment, and a risk-based test process as key concepts for risk-based testing, which are divided into several subcategories. For example, the degree of automation for the assessment of risk exposure is a concept below risk assessment.

Finally, Erdogan et al. [7] conducted a structured literature review of risk-based testing. They identified works concerned with model-based risk estimation, test case generation, test case analysis, source code analysis, measurements, specific programming paradigms and application domains. All in all, 24 approaches are categorized and presented in their literature review.

3   Production Usage Risk and Coverage

3.1   Regression Risk

A risk is defined as a possible (adverse) event. A risk R therefore consists of two components: the probability p that this event occurs and the damage D that is dealt in case of this event (see Eq. 1.)

$$R := p \cdot D \tag{1}$$

When releasing a new version of a software, there are risks concerning regressions. Regressions are newly introduced defects into parts of the system, which were already working properly and should work unchanged in the new software version.

From a user's point of view, the damage of such a regression is the impact on his/her work, i.e., his/her ability to execute the actions that are the driver to use the software. If many users have used the newly broken functionality up to the latest release, the higher the damage is from the user's perspective and as such for the software owner. We quantify this damage of the regression risk D_{RR} as the proportional amount of past executions E_p of a measured functionality $f \in F$ compared to all executions of all functionalities (see Eq. 2.)

$$D_{RR}(f, F, E_p) := \frac{|E_p(f)|}{|E_p(F)|} \tag{2}$$

A functionality $f \in F$ is a functionality of both the current production release as well as the to be released software system. The set of all functionalities $(F := \bigcup f_i)$ represents the whole functionality that is common to both systems. Because we are concerned with regressions, functionalities in F need to be both available in the latest productive version n of the software system as well as still present in the new version $n + 1$, thus, $F := F_n \cap F_{n+1}$. If a functionality is only present in the newest version ($f \notin F_n \wedge f \in F_{n+1}$) it is a newly added functionality, which is not subject to regression tests. If it is only present in the previous version ($f \notin F_n \wedge f \notin F_{n+1}$) it has been removed in the newest version and is therefore not subject to future regression testing.

The more frequently a functionality is used, the more damage is dealt from a user's perspective if that functionality is broken. In the extremes this means on the one hand that if a functionality, which is never used, is broken by a regression, no one will notice and no harm is done. Thus, the damage and consequently the risk is zero. If on the other hand, the broken functionality is the only one used, all other aspects of the software can be working perfectly but no user will be able to use the system anymore. The damage – and consequently the risk – is very high in the this case.

The probability of a change leading to a regression is influenced first and foremost by whether the functionality is affected by the change or not. If it is not, i.e., no changed software artefact is executed as part of executing a functionality, we assume that the software is still working correctly and thus the probability is zero (see Eq. 3). If the functionality depends on changed code, the probability is $0 < p_F \leq 1$ because the introduced change might or might not break the functionality. The probability of breaking existing functionality is influenced by several factors like change size, complexity of the changed code etc. In order to build a model that can be used in practice, we simplify this by assuming a constant probability 1 for a regression for every software change.

$$p(f) := \begin{cases} 0 & \text{no code change in f} \\ 1 & \text{code change in f} \end{cases} \tag{3}$$

Regression Risk RR is defined by substituting the adapted damage (Eq. 2) and probability (Eq. 3) into the risk definition (Eq. 1) resulting in Eq. 4. Because software consists of many functionalities, the overall regression risk is the sum of all regression risks of all functionalities $f \in F$.

$$RR(F, E_p) := \sum_{f \in F} (p(f) \cdot |E_p(f)|) \tag{4}$$

3.2   Regression Risk Coverage

By knowing the regression risk of a code change, a coverage definition can be defined: regression risk coverage indicates to what extend regression tests have addressed the regression risk for the current release.

As with all coverage metrics, the formula describes the relationship of covered objects with regards to all objects. Usually, these are simple counts (e.g. covered vs. total statements/branches/...). However, in our case this is the covered risk, i.e., the risk addressed by the executions E_t of the tests vs. the whole risk by the productive executions E_p of the system as shown in Eq. 5.

$$RRC(F, E_p, E_t) := \frac{RR(F, E_t \cap E_p)}{RR(F, E_p)} \tag{5}$$

In order to measure regression risk coverage, we need to know the functionalities of a system F (both present in the productive and in the newest version), past executions on the productive system E_p and executions during the test E_t. Note that the proportion is not directly calculated with the functionalities covered during test, but only those functionalities that are present covered during regression tests and in production ($E_t \cap E_p$).

3.3   Partitioning a System into Functionalities

Calculating Regression Risk and Regression Risk Coverage requires a partitioning of the system into functionalities. Like with other coverage metrics, different options are available to use as objects to measure for calculating the metrics.

A suitable set of functionalities F have to fulfil the following requirements. They must be

Distinct: Functionalities are a partition. As such they must not overlap and an execution must be clearly assignable to one functionality: practically, a functionality f_j must not always be covered if another functionality f_i is covered: $\nexists i, j, i \neq j : E_p(f_i) > 0 \implies E_p(f_j) > 0$.
Complete: In order to test the whole system functionality, all partitions together must represent the whole functionality available to the user, i.e., there must be no execution which cannot be assigned to a functionality.
Measurable during Test: The execution of a functionality must be measurable during test. Like the measurement of established code coverage metrics, this can be achieved by multiple means, e.g., by instrumentation.
Measurable in Production: Besides being measurable during testing, execution must be measurable during production because the history of executions needs to be calculated. Usually, instrumentation is deemed to be too expensive run-time wise and should be avoided or minimized as much as possible [34]. Thus, other sources – like event logs or log files – might be more appropriate to use. The domain of business process mining [1] offers many techniques that are suitable to analyze high-level executions in software systems; although these techniques are usually only applied in order to better understand the business side (e.g., for deriving business metrics or documentation).
Mappable between Software Versions: Because measurements done in the production system are made against an older software version than the one, which is subject to regression testing, it must be possible to measure a functionality in both systems or to map executions within both systems to the same set of functionalities.

Although in general, metrics measured at the code level could be used, it seems questionable if this is a suitable way in practice, because the involved run-time penalty is high and the mapping between execution traces of changed code is difficult.

However, more high-level abstractions can be used. These include – but are not limited to:

- User Interactions and corresponding equivalence classes of user inputs,
- Log Statements that are already written and can – for example if developers apply log-based testing – replace instrumentation because the flow in the software can be measured by analyzing the log files,
- Event Logs that are utilized by modern event-driven architectures and offer a persistent trace of business-related events, which are already gathered by the software system(s),
- Process Execution Traces, which are written by business process management systems in order to offer the capability of process audits and rewinds. Such logs are so detailed that they can be used to calculate code-level coverage [21].

Within the case study presented below we define the sequencing of functionality in form of business process traces. By analyzing the (process) event logs of the application, we construct end-to-end traces of business processes.

A trace is the ordering of executed activities for achieving a goal. If the application is (a) event-based, i.e., the communication between its components is implemented by exchanging events that are made persistent in order to replay event streams, or (b) orchestration-based with a central workflow engine or business process management system, which writes an execution log of executed activities, such traces can be constructed. The latter applies to our case study project.

3.4 Use Cases for Regression Test Risk Coverage

Being able to measure Regression Risk RR and its Coverage RRC, allows members of software projects and especially the testers to benefit from this information in several ways:

Select Regression Tests for Execution: Complex systems with large regression test suites can require more time to execute than is available. In order to select the test cases to be run, the ones with most regression risk coverage can be selected so that a certain regression risk threshold is reached.

Prioritize Regression Test Development: Today's software systems are complex, thus requiring many regression tests to cover the systems. These need to be developed, which can be a time-consuming task, especially if an already existing system is to be complemented by regressions tests, or if the existing regression test suite is to be made more complete. By measuring the Regression Risk RR of such systems allows prioritizing the creation of regression tests in order to incrementally improve the achieved regression risk coverage.

Prioritize Regression Test Execution: Complex systems require a large set of regression tests in order to find as many regressions as possible for a software release. Naturally, running more test cases takes more time to complete. In order to prioritize test cases, they can be run in order of their Regression

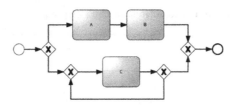

Fig. 1. A sample process

Risk. This leads to high-impact defects being found earlier and thus giving developers more time to fix them.

Evaluate Covered Risk by Regression Testing for a Software Release: Before a release is deployed into production, regression risk coverage can be calculated as a means to judge which parts of the system is untested weighted by the number of user interactions. If coverage is too low, quality managers and/or project managers can decide to postpone the release.

Evaluate Covered Risk by Regression Test Suite: Independent of a concrete release – and thus of a concrete change set – regression risk coverage of a regression test suite can show how well a project can accommodate future, unknown changes and is able to help guarding against regressions in frequently used functionalities.

One main advantage of this approach is that it is fully automatable, i.e., if applied in risk-based testing the risk assessment can be made automatically thereby saving time and effort.

4   Example

In order to demonstrate the regression risk and regression risk coverage metrics, we analyze a simple flow through a software system. This system is modelled as a BPMN (Business Process Model and Notation) process in Fig. 1.

This process has – due to the contained loop – an endless number of possible end-to-end traces. Thus, in theory we can construct as many test cases as we like because perhaps the software might fail at the next loop iteration.

By analyzing the events emitted from the software system we can compute how often different traces were executed in the productive system. We assume that users of the productive system have used the software system in the variants as shown in Table 1.

If new regression tests are to be implemented – or existing regression tests are to be executed – they should address the highest risk first. If A, B & C have been changed since the latest release, the trace A, B should be covered first ($RR = \frac{100}{200} = 0.5$), followed by the trace C, C ($RR = \frac{90}{200} = 0.45$) and finally C ($RR = \frac{10}{200} = 0.05$).

Also existing regression tests can be evaluated for how representative they are with regards to the behaviour of the users. If the regression test suite covers A,

Table 1. Executions of the sample process

Execution	Trace	E_p	Relative Usage
A → B	A,B	100	50%
C	C	10	5%
C → C	C,C	90	45%

B, C, and C, C, C, 55% of user interactions are covered and thus the regression risk coverage is $RRC = \frac{100+10+0}{200} = 0.55$. The test case that covers C, C, C does not add to the regression risk coverage because this trace has not been executed in the production release.

5 Case Study: Application in an Industrial Project

Within this section, a case study in an industrial project is presented, which was conducted in order to gain understanding of the practical application of regression risk coverage.

This section is structured according to the suggestion presented by Runeson et al. [37], which are in turn composed of the suggestions by Jedlitschka and Pfahl [14] and Kitchenham et al. [17].

5.1 Case Study Design

Research Questions. We conduct this case study because we want to answer the following research questions:

RQ1: Is the regression risk and regression risk coverage approach applicable in industry projects? This question validates whether regression risk and regression risk coverage can be measured in industry projects or not. This especially includes whether all data can be gathered economically and – in the best case – automatically. Because the field of process mining and log analysis has been researched well and the project uses a central process management system, which collects a full audit trail of executed activities, we assume that we can gather all data efficiently.

RQ2: What is the distribution of the occurrences of event traces? This question validates whether the chosen approach adds value for prioritizing the creation of new test cases or ordering the execution of existing test cases or not. If all functionalities are used more or less equally often, no gains can be achieved by applying this metric. We assume that a small number of common cases represent the most often used functionalities. The number of additionally required test cases should increase exponentially when increasing regression risk coverage. We hypothesize that more than 80% of regression risk coverage can be achieved by covering less than 50% of all functionalities encountered in the production system.

Case & Subject Selection. The motivation of this work came from the same project, which serves as the subject of the case study for applying the regression risk approach: Terravis [28] is a Swiss platform for integrating mortgage-related business processes end-to-end in a fully digitized manner. Therefore, different parties, including land registries, banks, and notaries are integrated via their systems allowing them to conduct relevant processes fully digitally. Today, most mortgage transactions in Switzerland are done via this platform and, when completely finalized, Terravis will connect more than 1000 partner systems.

Because the Terravis platform grew since its inception and the number of supported business process types as well as the supported variants in each of those increased, quality assurance in general and testing in particular have been a challenge [3]. Like probably all complex software systems, processes in Terravis are regularly updated and changed [19].

In order to efficiently test business processes, Terravis has used BPELUnit [27] from the beginning in order to conduct fully automated unit tests of the implemented processes. In order to improve the scope of the tests, system tests have been implemented by following a Behavior-Driven Approach, which builds upon BPMN models and generates BPELUnit tests, which drive the tests [24]. In the next step, unit test creation was improved by generating test suites with Combinatorial Test Design (CTD) and IPOG-C and AETG-SAT selection algorithms [5,18] in the project [22].

All these existing test types were driven by running SOAP message sequences (also for human task management) against the executable process models and services. Thus, the test drivers take the perspective of a partner that has integrated its systems with Terravis. However, the next step for the project was to implement fully automated user interface (UI) tests. Terravis offers a Web-based user interface, which can be used by notaries and banks for operating the processes. Although Terravis encourages partners to integrate their systems with the platform in order to realize the full benefits of end-to-end digital processing, some partners choose to use the Web interface instead, which was not covered by extensive regression test automation before.

When starting the implementation of regression tests for a large system, it is necessary to prioritize, which test cases to create first and to assess how many test cases are to be developed to build an efficient regression test suite.

Together with the project's test team, it was decided to prioritize frequently used business process variants in order to address the risk of regressions. Without acquiring additional infrastructure, e.g., additional servers for running tests, the maximum test running time available after the nightly build is approximately six hours. The project's goal is to cover as much regression risk as possible in the available time slot. Thus, the goal is to *select* the most efficient regression test cases.

During our research the project introduced a change to five of its supported processes: For banks that let a trustee manage their mortgages, a preview function of generated contracts and orders was to be implemented.

Table 2. Meta data of the process models (1) (according to Lübke et al. [23])

Process Name:	A: New Mortgage	B: Increase Mortgage	C: Generic Mortgage Business
Version:		—	
Domain:		Land Register Mortgage Transactions	
Geography:		Switzerland	
Time:		2019-03	
Boundary:		Cross-Organizational	
Relationships:		Calls another	
Scope:		Core	
Process Model Purpose:		Execution	
People Involvement:		None	
Process Language:		WS-BPEL 2.0 (w/ vendor extensions)	
Execution Engine:		ActiveVOS 9.2	
Model Maturity:		Productive	
NOA bef/aft:	332 / 344	409 / 418	248 / 254
Non-Linear Act. bef/aft:	145 / 151	186 / 191	78 / 82

The process implementations are modeled as WS-BPEL processes, which consists of 1373 basic activities prior to the change and 1420 basic activities after the change. Also the number of non-linear activities, i.e., those which split or join the control-flow (e.g., loops or conditions) rose from 544 to 573 with the new release. For a complete metadata description the reader is referred to Tables 2 and 3, which structure the process meta data according to the process template suggested for empirical research by Lübke et al [23].

Table 3. Meta data of the process models (2) (according to Lübke et. al [23])

Process Name:	D: Remove Mortgage from Trustee	E: Add Mortgage to Trustee
Version:	—	
Domain:	Trustee Mortgage Transactions	
Geography:	Switzerland	
Time:	2019-03	
Boundary:	Cross-Organizational	
Relationships:	Calls another	
Scope:	Core	
Process Model Purpose:	Execution	
People Involvement:	None	
Process Language:	WS-BPEL 2.0 (w/ vendor extensions)	
Execution Engine:	ActiveVOS 9.2	
Model Maturity:	Productive	
NOA bef/aft:	267 / 277	117 / 127
Non-Linear Act. bef/aft:	101 / 108	34 / 41

Data Collection Procedures. Because the case study project is centered around business process integration and automation, we decided to use distinct event traces as exemplified in Sect. 4 in end-to-end process instances for partitioning the system's functionality.

In the first iteration, the process logs of all completed processes in the production system, which were (a) started since the last release and (b) subject to modification in the new release, were analyzed and end-to-end traces were constructed along with their usage frequencies. The calculation was done with a small Java program, which had direct access to the event log in a relational database.

Analysis & Validity Procedures. For gathering and analyzing the required data, we needed to write a small program, which reads all process event logs from the production database and creates usage frequencies for the different end-to-end traces. The output was grouped by process and sorted by the trace's/functionality's usage frequency. This information is written into CSV files and later visualized by using R.

In order to maintain internal validity, we tested the program intensively and manually verified the output for a subset of process instances.

5.2   Results

Measurements. We wrote the program for analyzing the event logs from the business process management system, which meant reading and aggregating data from a relational database.

As described an (end-to-end) trace of business process serves as a functionality. End-to-end traces fulfil all outlined requirements for functionalities as described in Sect. 3.3. Thus, we use (end-to-end) trace and functionality as synonyms in this case study.

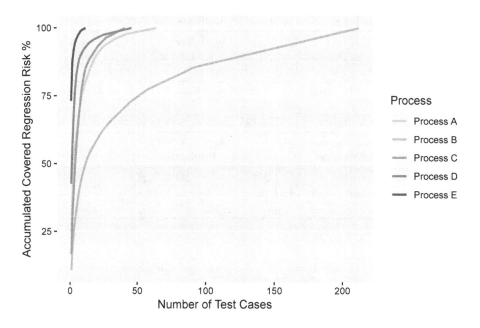

Fig. 2. Maximal regression risk coverage with increasing test case count

In total, we identified 3381 end-to-end traces of process instances and calculated their frequencies. The computation took approx. 3 h.

When creating test suites by taking the test cases, which cover the most additional functionality executions in production, the efficiency drops with additional test cases as shown in Fig. 2. While the first test cases cover many executions on the production system, the curves flatten out towards full coverage.

For better demonstrating the required test cases and covered execution traces, the numbers are shown in Table 4 for different regression risk coverage goals. For each process and all processes combined the number of required test cases for individual regression risk coverage levels (80%, 90%, 95%, 99% & 100%) alongside the number of covered production traces are shown in this table.

Additionally, the feedback of the testers was that the data was helpful for them in order to define, which regression tests to automate and in which order these should be implemented.

Table 4. Required test cases for achieving a defined regression risk coverage

Process	80% Goal		90% Goal		95% Goal		99% Goal		100% Goal	
	#TC	#Tr.	#TC	#Tr.	#TC	#Tr.	#TC	#Tr.	#TC	#Tr.
A	12	778	21	879	31	922	55	960	64	969
B	69	666	129	749	171	791	204	824	212	832
C	10	312	17	350	25	370	38	385	41	388
D	5	684	9	749	16	786	38	819	46	827
E	2	320	3	335	5	350	9	362	12	365
Total	98	2760	179	3062	248	3219	344	3350	375	3381

Interpretation

RQ1: Is the regression risk and regression risk coverage approach applicable in industry projects? Calculating regression risk and regression risk coverage was possible in the case study industry project. However, this was done by analyzing large event logs written by the Business Process Management System. The calculation needed to be written from scratch and evaluating the metrics was an hour-long process. This means that evaluating the baseline for the metrics, i.e., the types and numbers of past execution traces, needs to be actualized independently of the build. In the case study's case, this was a one-time activity although it is probably better to actualize it regularly in order to reflect changed user behavior.

RQ2: What is the distribution of the occurrences of event traces? Analyzing the number and distribution of event traces of the case study's project with regards to the analyzed change yields a clear non-linear distribution: it is relatively easy to cover an overall regression risk of 80% for the implemented change with 98 test cases. Covering all functionalities (i.e., execution traces) encountered in the productive system, in contrast requires 375 test cases. This means that a 20% increase of coverage can only be achieved by creating 3.8 times more test cases. Increasing coverage "only" to 90% still requires 179 test cases, which approximately doubles the number of test cases required for an 80% coverage. The required test cases to go from a 99% to a 100% level are nearly one additional test case for one additional covered end-to-end trace. Thus, the occurrence of the least used end-to-end traces is always only 1. This means that the regression risk coverage metric can be used in order to select and/or to prioritize regression test cases and thereby reducing the required run-time of regression tests while testing the important features from the point of the users. Setting a threshold for the regression tests to a fixed percentage or by looking at the individual frequency distribution and set a cut-off, projects can regression test their releases more economically and efficiently. However, the collected data also indicates that while the relative test case count, which is required for achieving a certain coverage level, is comparably stable, the absolute number of test cases differs by business processes, i.e., by the implementing software component. Process B is the largest process in terms of size (basic activities) and complexity (process branches and joins) and requires significantly more test cases to achieve a certain coverage level than any other of the changed processes in the analyzed release. With this knowledge (and according to the testers' feedback), projects can easily select and prioritize regression test cases by applying regression risk coverage.

Evaluation of Validity. Like with every other single-project case study, the question of generalizability arises. We have identified three major risks for external validity with our chosen research design:

1. Within the case study project the damage is very similar independent of the software component or issue. Other systems are different in this regards, e.g., there are safety components that are to be tested more intensively. A car's airbag might (hopefully) not be used frequently, but would be critical to be tested. Projects with such requirements cannot use this approach but need to complement it with defect costs or by treating system components individually and applying regression risk coverage to each of those and prioritize components separately.
2. Other projects might work differently, and have a different distribution of interactions with their users and partner systems. By only studying one project there is an inherent risk that some of the project's characteristics skew the results. In this case this might especially be the case for the implementation technology. If not using a Business Process Management System, the availability of data and/or the granularity of possible tracing into the productive application might be more difficult or impossible.
3. The selection of changed business processes and thus functionalities is homogeneous: All affected business processes were main end-to-end processes as shown in the classification tables. It has been shown by Lübke et al. [23] different categories of process properties can lead to statistically different behavior. They demonstrated that different process types exhibit different run-time behavior and have different control-flow complexities on average. It is possible that also the distribution of usage frequencies varies between different categories, although this has not been researched yet.

6   Conclusions and Outlook

6.1   Conclusions

Within this paper Regression Risk and Regression Risk Coverage have been proposed and defined in order to guide the creation and execution of regression test cases. The underlying idea is to measure the possible damage of a change by the number of user interactions of the past with the affected functionality. The more user interactions would be negatively affected under the new release due to a regression, the worse this regression is. In order to cover most of this damage, the Regression Risk Coverage metric can be used for judging what amount of past productive user interactions are replicated during regression tests.

Although the idea in itself is relatively simple, data gathering and analysis for the implementation requires the use of elaborate log analysis techniques in order to calculate the current user behaviour with the productive system.

For validating that it is possible to measure and apply the proposed metrics, they have been successfully applied in an industry project. The project's goal was to measure the impact of a release and to find the most important regression tests to automate in a test time-constraint environment.

The application was successful and as such the Regression Risk Coverage can be used as a stand-alone tool or in conjunction with other techniques for helping testers to select and prioritize regression tests. It was shown that the business processes of this project have very dominant variants so that a 80% Regression Risk Coverage can be achieved within the given short test execution time window, which was available for nightly automated tests.

6.2   Possible Future Work

Applying Regression Risk Coverage in the industry project has revealed some open questions, which can be addressed in future research.

Most importantly, the question on analyzing the user interactions from productions raises the question of the time-frame to analyze. We found that differences in the duration of business process variants can make data not representative. While we used the time from the last release in our application, ideas to use a fixed 0.5 or 1 year period came up. However, in order to implement this idea, the traces of multiple software versions need to be mapped so that a combined regression risk across all software versions can be calculated. (Semi-)Automating this step would be a beneficial next step for applying this technique further.

Also the presented technique can in theory be used in conjunction with other selection and/or prioritization strategies. Making empirical studies about which combinations are the most effective and/or provide most coverage is a valuable next research goal. For example, combining usage frequencies and (estimated) costs for a defect might make this approach more general applicable.

The industry project has used the new metrics for one new release, which was comparatively large. Thus, most user interactions in the changed business processes were affected by this change. Further research can therefore explore what a typical regression risk for a change is and what constitutes influencing factors. For example, small releases in a two-week agile sprint should likely carry a lower regression risk compared to large releases.

Within this paper we laid the foundation for pursuing these additional questions. We therefore hope that our work is useful for other projects and researchers alike in order to utilize usage data for better selecting and prioritizing regression test cases!

References

1. van der Aalst, W.: Process Mining - Data Science in Action. Springer, Heidelberg (2016). https://doi.org/10.1007/978-3-662-49851-4
2. Ansari, A., Khan, A., Khan, A., Mukadam, K.: Optimized regression test using test case prioritization. Procedia Comput. Sci. **79**, 152–160 (2016)
3. Berli, W., Lübke, D., Möckli, W.: Terravis - large scale business process integration between public and private partners. In: Plödereder, E., Grunske, L., Schneider, E., Ull, D. (eds.) Proceedings INFORMATIK 2014. Lecture Notes in Informatics (LNI), vol. P-232, pp. 1075–1090. Gesellschaft für Informatik e.V., Gesellschaft für Informatik e.V. (2014)
4. Bertolino, A.: Software testing research: achievements, challenges, dreams. In: 2007 Future of Software Engineering, pp. 85–103. IEEE Computer Society (2007)
5. Cohen, D.M., Dalal, S.R., Fredman, M.L., Patton, G.C.: The AETG system: an approach to testing based on combinatorial design. IEEE Trans. Softw. Eng. **23**(7), 437–444 (1997). https://doi.org/10.1109/32.605761
6. Cohen, D.M., Dalal, S.R., Parelius, J., Patton, G.C.: The combinatorial design approach to automatic test generation. IEEE Softw. **13**(5), 83–88 (1996)
7. Erdogan, G., Li, Y., Runde, R.K., Seehusen, F., Stølen, K.: Approaches for the combined use of risk analysis and testing: a systematic literature review. Int. J. Softw. Tools Technol. Transf. **16**(5), 627–642 (2014). https://doi.org/10.1007/s10009-014-0330-5
8. Felderer, M., Schieferdecker, I.: A taxonomy of risk-based testing. Int. J. Softw. Tools Technol. Transf. **16**(5), 559–568 (2014). https://doi.org/10.1007/s10009-014-0332-3
9. Go, K., Kang, S., Baik, J., Kim, M.: Pairwise testing for systems with data derived from real-valued variable inputs. Softw. Pract. Exp. **46**(3), 381–403 (2016)
10. Gonzalez-Sanchez, A., Piel, É., Abreu, R., Gross, H.G., van Gemund, A.J.: Prioritizing tests for software fault diagnosis. Softw. Pract. Exp. **41**(10), 1105–1129 (2011)
11. Graves, T.L., Harrold, M.J., Kim, J.M., Porter, A., Rothermel, G.: An empirical study of regression test selection techniques. ACM Trans. Softw. Eng. Methodol. (TOSEM) **10**(2), 184–208 (2001)
12. Harrold, M.J.: Testing: a roadmap. In: Proceedings of the Conference on The Future of Software Engineering, ICSE 2000, pp. 61–72. ACM, New York (2000). https://doi.org/10.1145/336512.336532. http://doi.acm.org/10.1145/336512.336532
13. Hertis, M., Juric, M.B.: An empirical analysis of business process execution language usage. IEEE Trans. Software Eng. **40**(08), 738–757 (2014)
14. Jedlitschka, A., Pfahl, D.: Reporting guidelines for controlled experiments in software engineering. In: 2005 International Symposium on Empirical Software Engineering, p. 10. IEEE (2005)
15. Kim, J.M., Porter, A.: A history-based test prioritization technique for regression testing in resource constrained environments. In: Proceedings of the 24th International Conference on Software Engineering, ICSE 2002, pp. 119–129. ACM, New York (2002). https://doi.org/10.1145/581339.581357. http://doi.acm.org/10.1145/581339.581357

16. Kim, S., Baik, J.: An effective fault aware test case prioritization by incorporating a fault localization technique. In: Proceedings of the 2010 ACM-IEEE International Symposium on Empirical Software Engineering and Measurement, p. 5. ACM (2010)
17. Kitchenham, B.A., Pfleeger, S.L., Pickard, L.M., Jones, P.W., Hoaglin, D.C., El Emam, K., Rosenberg, J.: Preliminary guidelines for empirical research in software engineering. IEEE Trans. Softw. Eng. **28**(8), 721–734 (2002)
18. Lei, Y., Kacker, R., Kuhn, D.R., Okun, V., Lawrence, J.: IPOG-IPOG-D: efficient test generation for multi-way combinatorial testing. Softw. Test. Verif. Reliab. **18**(3), 125–148 (2008). https://doi.org/10.1002/stvr.v18:3
19. Lübke, D.: Using metric time lines for identifying architecture shortcomings in process execution architectures. In: 2015 IEEE/ACM 2nd International Workshop on Software Architecture and Metrics (SAM), pp. 55–58. IEEE (2015)
20. Lübke, D.: Extracting and conserving production data as test cases in executable business process architectures. In: Cruz-Cunha, M.M., et al. (eds.) Proceedings of CENTERIS 2017 (2017)
21. Lübke, D.: An extended evaluation of process log analysis for BPEL test coverage calculation. Int. J. Adv. Syst. Meas. **11**(3&4) (2018)
22. Lübke, D., Greenyer, J., Vatlin, D.: Effectiveness of combinatorial test design with executable business processes. Empirical Studies on the Development of Executable Business Processes, pp. 199–223. Springer, Cham (2019). https://doi.org/10.1007/978-3-030-17666-2_9
23. Lübke, D., Ivanchikj, A., Pautasso, C.: A template for categorizing empirical business process metrics. In: Carmona, J., Engels, G., Kumar, A. (eds.) Business Process Management Forum - BPM Forum 2017 (2017)
24. Lübke, D., van Lessen, T.: Modeling test cases in BPMN for behavior-driven development. IEEE Softw. 17–23 (2016)
25. Lübke, D., Unger, T., Wutke, D.: Analysis of data-flow complexity and architectural implications. Empirical Studies on the Development of Executable Business Processes, pp. 59–81. Springer, Cham (2019). https://doi.org/10.1007/978-3-030-17666-2_4
26. Marijan, D., Gotlieb, A., Liaaen, M.: A learning algorithm for optimizing continuous integration development and testing practice. Softw. Pract. Exp. **49**(2), 192–213 (2019)
27. Mayer, P., Lübke, D.: Towards a BPEL unit testing framework. In: TAV-WEB 2006: Proceedings of the 2006 Workshop on Testing, Analysis, and Verification of Web Services and Applications, Portland, USA, pp. 33–42. ACM Press, New York (2006). http://doi.acm.org/10.1145/1145718.1145723, http://portal..acm.org/affiliated/citation.cfm?id=1145718.1145723&coll=ACM&dl=ACM&type=series&idx=1145718&part=Proceedings&WantType=Proceedings&title=International%20Symposium%20on%20Software%20Testing%20and%20Analysis&CFID=1483183&CFTOKEN=32880799#
28. Möckli, W., Lübke, D.: Terravis - the case of process-oriented land register transactions digitization. In: Digital Government Excellence Awards 2017: An Anthology of Case Histories. ACPIL (2017)
29. Mukherjee, R., Patnaik, K.S.: A survey on different approaches for software test case prioritization. J. King Saud Univ. Comput. Inf. Sci. (2018)
30. Myers, G.J., Sandler, C.: The Art of Software Testing, 2nd edn. Wiley, Chichester (2004)
31. Pan, J.: Software testing. Dependable Embed. Syst. **5**, 2006 (1999)

32. Panda, S., Mohapatra, D.P.: Regression test suite minimization using integer linear programming model. Softw. Pract. Exp. **47**(11), 1539–1560 (2017)
33. Park, H., Ryu, H., Baik, J.: Historical value-based approach for cost-cognizant test case prioritization to improve the effectiveness of regression testing. In: 2008 Second International Conference on Secure System Integration and Reliability Improvement, pp. 39–46, July 2008. https://doi.org/10.1109/SSIRI.2008.52
34. Pavlopoulou, C., Young, M.: Residual test coverage monitoring. In: Proceedings of the 21st International Conference on Software Engineering, ICSE 1999, pp. 277–284. ACM, New York (1999). https://doi.org/10.1145/302405.302637. http://doi.acm.org/10.1145/302405.302637
35. Rothermel, G., Harrold, M.J.: Analyzing regression test selection techniques. IEEE Trans. Softw. Eng. **22**(8), 529–551 (1996)
36. Rothermel, G., Harrold, M.J.: A safe, efficient regression test selection technique. ACM Trans. Softw. Eng. Methodol. **6**(2), 173–210 (1997). https://doi.org/10.1145/248233.248262. http://doi.acm.org/10.1145/248233.248262
37. Runeson, P., Höst, M., Rainer, A., Regnell, B.: Case Study Research in Software Engineeering - Guidelines and Examples. Wiley, Hoboken (2012)
38. Shihab, E., Jiang, Z.M., Adams, B., Hassan, A.E., Bowerman, R.: Prioritizing the creation of unit tests in legacy software systems. Softw. Pract. Exp. **41**(10), 1027–1048 (2011)
39. Wong, W.E., Horgan, J.R., London, S., Mathur, A.P.: Effect of test set minimization on fault detection effectiveness. Softw. Pract. Exp. **28**(4), 347–369 (1998)

An Evaluation of Test Suite Minimization Techniques

Raphael Noemmer[1(✉)] and Roman Haas[2]

[1] Technical University of Munich, Munich, Germany
noemmer@cqse.eu
[2] CQSE GmbH, Munich, Germany

Abstract. As a software project evolves over time, the associated test suite usually grows with it. If test suites are not carefully maintained, this can easily result in massive test execution duration, reducing the benefits of regression testing because faults are found later in development or even after release. Test suite minimization aims to combat long running test suites by removing redundant test cases. Previous work mainly evaluates test suite minimization techniques based on comparably small projects, which are less practically relevant. In this paper, we compare four test suite minimization techniques by applying them to several open source software projects and evaluate the results. We find that the size and execution time of all the test suites can be reduced by over 70% on average. However, there is a substantial loss in fault detection capability of, on average, around 12.5%, restricting the applicability of this form of test suite minimization.

1 Introduction

The size of test suites tends to grow over time, which leads to an increasing amount of time used for each test run [5]. Test suites of large projects may run for days or even weeks. This is problematic for continuous integration where tests are ideally executed after every commit to give feedback to the developers as early as possible. The delay of feedback makes it harder to fix failures found by the tests because the changes might have been made several days ago, requiring the developer to refamiliarize himself with the changed code. Besides, more changes might have been made to the same code since the tests have started running. Additionally, there is a lot more changed code at once, making it harder to identify the fault that is the root cause of test failures. In the literature, three research areas, coping with long running test suites, can be found. The first approach is *Test case selection* where test cases to be executed are chosen depending on the changes made since the last test run. Because unit tests cover specific areas of a system and, in general, changes over a limited time span are

This work was partially funded by the German Federal Ministry of Education and Research (BMBF), grant "SOFIE, 01IS18012A". The responsibility for this article lies with the authors.

limited to parts of a system, it is usually not necessary to execute all test cases every time. The main difficulty of this approach is to identify, which test case runs through which code after changes have been made. To get this information precisely, the whole test suite would need to run again, rendering the test selection approach useless. Usually, heuristics, based on test coverage data from earlier test runs, are used to resolve this issue. The second option is *test case prioritization*. In contrast to the other approaches, it does not aim for run time reduction of test suites but instead for a faster fault detection. With this method, test cases are executed in order of their relevance for the changes made. This can be accomplished by executing fast test cases that cover changes first. So, with this approach, the whole test suite is still executed, but the tests that are executed first have the highest likelihood of finding faults. This allows for the developers to get quick feedback without any loss in the overall fault detection. The last approach, and the one we are using in this paper, is *test suite minimization*. Test suite minimization attempts to find redundant tests that have little to no impact on fault detection capabilities of a test suite and remove them permanently. There are several common ways of determining whether a test is redundant, that is, has a low likelihood of detecting faults which are not found by the remaining tests. For determining the redundancy of a test, one or multiple criteria can be used, for example, statement coverage, execution cost, mutation coverage, mc/dc coverage etc. The tests that satisfy the chosen criteria are then selected and the rest is removed, ideally leading to a permanent reduction in the runtime of a test suite.

Problem Statement. In many software projects, regression testing takes up large amounts of time which can slow down development. Test suite minimization can be used to reduce the time each test run takes by removing redundant test cases. However, test suite minimization is rarely used in practice. We identified two core reasons for this, the first of which is that it is not an easy task to perform, especially with complex builds. The second reason is that removing test cases always carries the risk of reducing the effectiveness of the test suite. Due to the nature of test suite minimization, tests are usually removed permanently, which is a risk that has to be taken compared to test case selection or prioritization.

Contribution. In this paper, we evaluate different algorithms for test suite minimization with seven open source projects and make the following contributions:

- *Random Mutation Testing for Evaluation*
  A lot of the papers on test suite reduction utilize manually introduced faults in their underlying research for the evaluation of the loss in fault detection capability. By using mutation testing instead, we can generate a higher number of faults, equally spread over the whole project, which allows us to assess fault detection capability at a larger scale.
- *Real Open Source Projects*
  For the evaluation of test suite minimization, small test projects that were published for research purpose only, are used [7,16]. We chose to use actively maintained open source projects which are developed by a variety of

organizations to investigate the applicability of test suite minimization techniques in practice.
– *Time Measurements of Minimized Test Suites*
  Test suite minimization approaches are often evaluated, based on the number of tests that could be removed from the original test suite. Although, this is a relevant statistic which we report as well, the biggest benefit of test suite minimization in practice is to save execution time. Since execution times for tests can vary a lot in practice, the time savings need to be considered separately from the number of tests. To find out whether the practical benefits of test suite reduction are proportional to the number of removed tests, we analyze execution times of test suite before and after minimization is applied.

2   Fundamentals

In the following, we describe two basic concepts in the field software testing that we need for our study. The first is a formal description of test suite minimization, a technique that aims to reduce the runtime of test suites by removing redundant tests, the second concept is mutation testing which can be used evaluating the fault detection capability of a test suite.

2.1   Test Suite Minimization

In their 2002 paper on test suite reduction, Rothermel et al. define the minimization problem as follows: Given a test suite T that contains test cases $t_1, t_2 \ldots t_n$ and requirements $r_1, r_2 \ldots r_n$ which can be satisfied by the test cases in T, find a minimal subset of T that satisfies the same requirements as T itself [13]. When all r_i need to be satisfied, the technique is called *adequate*. An *inadequate* approach means that some of the requirements may be left unsatisfied. The r_i can be different functional or structural requirements, for example line coverage or mutation coverage.

Selecting a minimal set of tests that satisfies the requirements means finding a minimal hitting subset of T over the r_i, which is an NP-complete problem. Due to this difficulty, heuristics are a compelling option. There are many different heuristics that have been used and analyzed for the purpose of test suite minimization [19] some of which we investigate in Sect. 3.

2.2   Mutation Testing

Mutation testing is a method of assessing a test suite where mutations, a set of simple changes, supposed to represent typical faults, are introduced into a system. The test suite is then rated based on how many of the introduced faults are detected [9]. These faults are called mutants, and finding one of them is called 'killing a mutant'. The score of a test suite is calculated as follows:

$$MutationScore = \frac{numberOfFoundMutants}{numberOfIntroducedMutants}$$

It has been shown that mutants are similar enough to real faults to allow the mutation score to give a good indication of the real-world fault detection capability of a test suite [1]. There are, however, some inherent flaws of mutation testing. It is, for example, possible for mutants to cancel each other out which leads to undetectable mutants. Mutations can also cause infinite loops which makes it hard to tell whether a test takes a long time or is stuck in an infinite loop.

3   Related Work

The test suite minimization algorithms most commonly found in research are variations of the greedy algorithm [3,10] which has been shown to be an effective heuristic for the minimal hitting set problem [11]. Two well-known extensions of the greedy algorithm are the GE (Greedy Essential) and GRE (Greedy Redundant Essential) algorithms. Chen and Lau compared these two greedy variants to another heuristic called HGS (Harrold-Gupta-Soffa) [3,6]. Their results suggested that, though there are differences, neither technique is better than the others in all cases. Tallam and Gupta invented another version of the greedy heuristic, the delayed greedy algorithm [15]. It avoids selecting test cases that may later be rendered redundant by other selected test cases. This can happen when large tests are selected early on but then the subsequently selected tests, together, cover the same requirements. To avoid it, they removed the test cases, whose coverage is either a subset of another test or is completely covered by multiple other tests. After the tests are removed, the normal greedy heuristic is applied.

Offut et al. used mutation testing but instead of evaluating the quality of the minimized test suite on the basis of the resulting mutation score [10], they used the score as a criterion for minimization, that is, the mutants are the requirements that need to be satisfied by the algorithm. They compared statement coverage to mutation score as testing requirements for minimization. Their mutation score was based on manually created mutants. In our study, we used automated mutation testing which allows for about two orders of magnitude more mutants. The automation also allows us to use larger projects.

There are also approaches that use more than one objective for test suite minimization. Selective redundancy is the approach used by Jeffrey and Gupta [7,8] in their multi objective approach. Selective redundancy means that, if a test is marked redundant by the first set of testing requirements, it is not removed until it is also redundant with respect to the second set of requirements. Only if a test is redundant for both sets of requirements, it is omitted. Gupta et al. used branch-coverage and all-uses coverage as their criteria. Their results showed less omitted tests but also an improvement to fault detection capability compared to the HGS heuristic with only one requirement.

Wei et al. also utilized mutation testing, but instead of evaluating their results with the mutation score, they used it as a goal for several different many-objective evolutionary algorithms [16]. These algorithms can be used to optimize many-objective problems with four or more conflicthing criterions. While this provides a good approach for selecting tests, the resulting mutation score is not comparable since tests are selected based on their mutation killing capability. They also employed smaller test suites compared to our study subjects.

Regarding the fault detection loss of test suites through minimization, there are conflicting results. While Rothermel et al. found significant losses in fault detection effectiveness of test suites through the use of minimization [12,13], Zhang et al. found only small losses in fault detection when using test suite reduction on the same projects from the Software-artifact Infrastructure Repository[1][20]. Wong et al. also found that the impact of test suite minimization on a test suite's ability to detect faults is negligible [17,18].

Shi et al. have taken a very similar approach to test suite reduction as we do in this paper [14]. They used mutation testing to evaluate 18 open source projects from GitHub. Their focus was on using the mutation score instead of line coverage as testing requirement for minimization. They also evaluated adequate and inadequate approaches and looked at different versions of the projects they investigated. They found that mutant-based minimization is better with regard to the fault detection loss while the statement-based approach delivers slightly better minimization results.

4   Implementation

Our goal in this paper is to investigate the applicability of test suite minimization techniques in practice. To achieve this, we implemented test suite minimization and a way to run mutation testing, as an indicator of fault detection capability, on the reduced test suites.

In Fig. 1, we provide a structural overview of how we evaluate our chosen test suite minimization algorithms. First, we recorded testwise coverage for the tests of a project, using a modified version of JaCoCo[2]. We need this testwise coverage to apply the coverage-based minimization algorithms we have chosen. For our evaluation, we used two algorithms, a greedy algorithm, and the HGS heuristic. The goal of both of these algorithms is to select a subset of tests that covers the same as the original test suite but with different approaches. For both of them, we used statement coverage as the testing requirements for minimization. We used both, an adequate and an inadequate approach for each of the two algorithms. The adequate approach selects test cases until all lines are covered while, for the inadequate approach, new tests are selected until they no longer contribute at least five lines of additional coverage to the chosen subset of tests.

---

[1] https://sir.csc.ncsu.edu/php/previewfiles.php.
[2] https://github.com/cqse/teamscale-jacoco-agent.

4.1   The Greedy Algorithm

The greedy algorithm selects test cases by iteratively choosing the test case with the most additional statement coverage. First, the test with the most overall coverage is selected, that is, the test case t_k that satisfies the most testing requirements r_i. The requirements $r_n \ldots r_m$ covered by this first test are then removed from the coverage of all other test cases. This means that for each $t_j, j \neq k$, the operation $\{r_y \ldots r_z\} \setminus \{r_n \ldots r_m\}$ where $r_y \ldots r_z$ are the requirements satisfied by t_j is performed. The result of the set-theoretic difference is the new set of requirements satisfied by t_j. With this, we optimize for additional coverage and ignore what has already been covered. New tests are selected according to this rule until no additional coverage can be achieved by selecting more tests. In case of the inadequate approach, the heuristics stops earlier, in our case when no more than five lines can be added by selecting an additional test case.

4.2   The HGS Algorithm

The HGS heuristic works by adding test cases based on their cardinality, starting with the tests that have the lowest cardinality. To determine the cardinality of test case t_j take all testing requirements $r_n \ldots r_m$ covered by test case t_j. For $r_n \ldots r_m$, check by how many test cases each r_i is covered. The requirement r_i with the lowest number of test cases covering it, is the cardinality of test case t_j. For the algorithm this means, we start with the lines that are only covered by one test case. This gives us a set of test cases. All these test cases need to be added since they are essential, that is, they are the only tests that cover some lines. We then proceed with requirements that are covered by two test cases and iteratively add the test case with the highest additional coverage. We add test cases one by one and go up in cardinality until all requirements are met.

4.3   Mutation Testing

After we have the full and minimized test suites, we use the mutation testing tool Pitest[3] on the resulting test suites to get an approximation of how well the fault detection capability is maintained after the minimization is applied. Pitest provides a list of mutators[4], most of which are active by default. Their goal is to emulate real faults as realistically as possible. The advantage of mutation testing is the number of faults we can introduce and the randomness of them. By using real-world projects instead of the fairly small projects from the Software-artifact Infrastructure Repository, which are often used in research on test suite reduction, we want to evaluate how well test suite minimization works in practice.

---

[3] http://pitest.org.
[4] http://pitest.org/quickstart/mutators/.

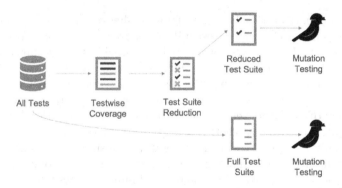

Fig. 1. Approach

5   Empirical Assessment

In this section, we want to examine the performance of statement coverage based test suite minimization. First, we describe our research questions followed by the subjects we chose to examine to answer said questions. We then explain, how we investigated each question and finally answer the questions according to the results we obtained.

5.1   Research Questions

The goal of our research is to find out how much our chosen test suite minimization techniques influence the fault revelation capability of test suites. Since the mutation score of a test suite is linked to its fault detection capability the resulting mutation score will give us an indication on how much the quality of a test suite suffers when minimization is used. With our experiments, we answer the following research questions.

RQ1 – How well is a test suite's capability to kill mutants preserved after test suite minimization is applied? Test suite minimization is only useful if a test suite preserves its fault detection capability through the process. We want to find out, if and how much worse a test suite gets at detecting faults, represented by mutants, when test suite minimization is used.

RQ2 – How much does the mutant killing capability vary between different test suite minimization techniques? We look at two different techniques to find out whether there is a considerable difference. We chose a simple greedy algorithm and compare it with a more complex algorithm, the HGS heuristic, to investigate how much of a difference using a more sophisticated algorithm, like the HGS, makes, compared to a simple greedy heuristic.

RQ3 – How does adequate test minimization perform compared to inadequate test minimization with a lower limit of five lines per test? Using adequate test suite minimization techniques means that even if it covers only one additional line, a test case has to be included in the set of tests.

With an inadequate approach, we can fix a number of minimum required newly covered lines and only include a test if it exceeds the lower limit. We expect this to reduce the number of tests considerably, improving the minimization result, but with five lines as the minimum number of newly covered lines, it might also have a substantial negative impact on the fault detection capability.

RQ4 – How big are the time savings and are they proportional to the number of omitted tests? The goal of test suite reduction is to save test execution time. To find out whether this goal is achieved, we analyze how much time is actually saved in a test run after applying test suite minimization. Since test cases can have vastly different runtime, we want to find out how much the runtime reduction is connected to the reduced number of tests and whether this behaves similarly in all study subjects.

5.2   Study Subjects

For our study, we examined seven systems, all of which are open source projects hosted on GitHub[5] and implemented in Java. We decided on Java because it is the only language supported by Pitest which is one of the most comprehensive and well maintained mutation testing tools we could find. The systems we chose vary in size from around 1k SLOC (Source Lines of Code) to 170k SLOC. We chose three projects from the Apache Software Foundation. They are well maintained, have a solid number of tests and are among our larger study subjects. With Ebean and Spoon, we included two other fairly large projects. To cover a wider set of different characteristics, we chose two smaller projects, JSoup, and Faux-pas, as well. All of our subject projects use Apache Maven as their build tool and use either JUnit version 4 or 5 for unit testing, which allows us to apply mutation testing (using Pitest) to their tests.

Table 1 shows a detailed overview of our subject projects. The LLOC (Logical Lines of Code) and coverage thereof are the numbers relevant for Pitest. For this value, only lines that can actually be executed are counted. For example, function headers and class declarations are not included in this metric. For mutation testing, only these lines are relevant since they are the ones that can potentially be mutated. For the SLOC metric, all lines that contain source code are counted, so only empty lines and comments are excluded. The number of mutants that are introduced is determined by Pitest according to the number of possible mutations.

Also note that the number of tests in Table 1 are the test cases that we executed. This number may be lower than the total number of tests in some instances because we removed or ignored tests that caused problems. These are, for the most part, tests that failed when running the test suite and some parametrized tests which cannot properly undergo test suite minimization.

5.3   Study Design

In this section, we describe, how we approached answering each of our research questions.

---
[5] https://github.com.

Table 1. Study subject details.

Study subjects	SLOC	SLOC project	SLOC test	LLOC Cov	#Tests	# Mutants
Commons Collection	62,897	28,708	34,189	46%	14,770	8,253
Commons Lang	75,408	27,825	47,583	95%	3,252	13,088
Commons Math	171,060	82,706	88,354	90%	4,825	37,674
Ebean	170,619	99,317	71,302	64%	2,598	25,056
Fauxpas	1,141	315	826	96%	81	50
JSoup	20,099	12,037	8,062	83%	666	4,711
Spoon	112,614	60,619	51,995	83%	1,608	15,887

RQ1 – How well is a test suite's capability to kill mutants preserved after test suite minimization is applied? To answer this question, we ran mutation testing on the original test suite and on the test suite minimized by the greedy algorithm for all our study subjects. We compare the mutation scores and calculate the relative mutation score loss from the minimization. Besides the timeout factor and constant, we used the default settings of Pitest. These factors were increased to reduce the number of false positive timeouts, a timeout is reported despite no infinite loop present. This increases the runtime but also increases the accuracy of the results we get.

RQ2 – How much does the mutant killing capability vary between different test suite minimization techniques? For our second research question, we ran the greedy and the HGS algorithm on our study subjects. We used mutation testing to find out how well the different minimization algorithms work with our study subjects and whether there is a significant difference between the techniques.

RQ3 – How does adequate test minimization compare to inadequate test minimization with a lower limit of five lines per test? For this, we use the same set-up as for RQ2 and additionally use inadequate versions of our algorithms. We compare the different approaches using mutation testing and their respective reduction in test suite size.

RQ4 – How much time can be saved per test run and are the time savings proportional to the number of omitted tests? To analyze, how much time is saved per run, we measure the run time of each test suite. We investigate both our algorithms in their adequate and inadequate forms. To minimize the possibility of background tasks influencing our results, we take five measurements for each project and minimization algorithm. We report the average reduction in execution time for each project's test suite.

6 Results and Discussion

In this section, we present and discuss the results of our experiments.

RQ1 – How well is a test suite's capability to kill mutants preserved after test suite minimization is applied?

In Table 2, we display the number of killed mutants as well as the number of tests before and after minimization. Our results for the reduction are closely related to the results in the 2014 paper on test suite minimization by Shi et al. [14] who applied a similar approach. Most of the projects have a reduction in test suite size from roughly 60% to 75% with the median at 67%. The difference between our results and the results in the other paper can most likely be attributed to the difference in project selection. We consider a reduction of more than 50% in all projects very high and it was particularly impressive to us that even for the small projects, we got a reduction in test suite size of more than half.

The number that sticks out the most in terms of the test reduction is the 93% of the Apache Commons Collections library. On closer inspection we found that a lot of the test cases of that project are focused on very few classes which leads to an extreme effectiveness of the minimization as well as a low overall mutations score. A hint to this can be found in the comparably low LLOC coverage in Table 1 even though the number of tests is very high. In cases like this, we ignore that the developer might have a reason for having many tests for a small section of code. Even though this usually means that the minimization is very effective, we have no way of knowing whether that code is particularly important or complex and requires more testing.

The most important column of the table, however, is the relative MS (mutation score) loss. Due to the fact that it ranges from 3.5% to 21% in our study, the effectiveness appears to be dependent on the project in question and is not strongly correlated with the size reduction percentage. Our results also show that the Apache Foundation projects facilitate test suite minimization a lot better than the other projects we tested. They have similar reduction rates to the other projects but at a substantially lower loss in mutation score.

Overall, while the reduction figures are promising, the loss in mutation coverage for some of the projects is quite high. Potentially missing 21% of faults is unacceptable in a lot of cases. These results suggest that a stricter set of testing requirements for minimization instead of only statement coverage could make sense. This would likely limit the number of missed mutants but also reduce the effectiveness of the minimization. Our results also show that there is potential for test suite minimization in big software projects that are actively maintained.

Table 2. Comparison Full test suite and minimized Greedy.

Study subjects	Full test suite			Minimized test suite				
	# Tests	# MK	MS	# Tests	# MK	MS	Reduct	Rel MS loss
Commons Collection	14,770	3,459	42%	960	3,145	38%	93%	9.5%
Commons Lang	3,252	11,285	86%	1,638	10,873	83%	50%	3.5%
Commons Math	4,825	29,721	79%	1,574	27,893	74%	67%	6,3%
Ebean	2,598	10,971	44%	811	9,565	38%	69%	21%
Fauxpas	81	47	94%	23	39	78%	72%	17%
JSoup	666	3,167	67%	240	2,660	56%	64%	16%
Spoon	1,608	11,229	71%	482	9,683	61%	70%	14%

RQ2 – How much does the mutant killing capability vary between different test suite minimization techniques?

In Table 3, we have listed the number of tests after minimization as well as the number of killed mutants for both algorithms. We also display the relative difference in the number of selected tests and mutant killing capability. Our main finding here is that the differences between the greedy and the HGS algorithm are very minute in terms of the number of retained tests as well their mutant killing capability.

We observe that the HGS algorithm retains slightly fewer tests than the greedy algorithm but the difference is at most around 3% and with a p value $\gg$ 0.05, the HGS algorithm is not significantly better than the greedy algorithm. In terms of their mutation score, neither algorithm is superior as they are very close for all study subjects and neither of the two consistently outperforms the other.

These results confirm the results that Shi et al. found [14] which indicate that the differences between the simple greedy algorithm and more sophisticated algorithms is minute. Though we have only tried two algorithms, we observe that the more expensive HGS heuristic does not result in a palpable benefit for any of our study subjects. Though, because of the nature of test suite minimization, the algorithm is only applied rarely, so a more time consuming, but slightly more effective algorithm might still be worth it.

Table 3. Comparison Greedy HGS.

Study subjects	Greedy		HGS			
	# Tests	# MK	# Tests	# MK	Rel test diff	Rel MS diff
Commons Collections	960	3, 145	943	3, 116	1.77%	0.92%
Commons Lang	1, 638	10, 873	1, 632	10, 883	0.37%	0.092%
Commons Math	1, 574	27, 893	1, 544	27, 574	1.91%	1.14%
Ebean	811	9, 565	799	9, 450	1.48%	1.20%
Fauxpas	23	39	23	41	0.0%	4.88%
JSoup	240	2, 660	233	2, 656	2.92%	0.15%
Spoon	482	9, 683	477	10, 123	1.04%	4.35%

RQ3 – How does adequate test minimization compare to inadequate test minimization with a lower limit of five lines per test?

We display our results for this question in Table 4. In the table, we can see that the benefits of using the inadequate technique are quite substantial. Compared to the adequate variants, the number of remaining tests is more than halfed for most of our study subjects. Of course, the overall impact is significantly lower with an absolute average decrease in the number of tests of 86.7% for the inadequate greedy algorithm compared to 69.2% for the adequate greedy algorithm. The HGS algorithm behaves very similar.

However, there is also a substantial drop in mutation score across most of our study subjects. For most of our projects, the drop in fault detection capability compared to the adequate version is considerably larger than the drop from the full test suite to the adequately minimized version. Compared to the adequate version, the inadequate minimization is not worthwile due to the lower absolute gain and the higher loss in fault detection capability.

There are different versions of inadequacy, for example we could also limit the overall coverage we want to achieve instead of introducing a lower limit per test.

Table 4. Comparison adequate inadequate

Study subjects	Greedy						Hgs					
	Adequate		Inadequate		Difference		Adequate		Inadequate		Difference	
	# Tests	# MK	# Tests	# MK	Tests	MS	# Tests	MS	# Tests	# MK	Tests	MS
Commons Collections	960	3,145	401	2,522	58%	19.8%	943	3,116	434	2,598	54%	16.6%
Commons Lang	1,638	10,873	662	9,201	60%	15.4%	1,632	10,883	691	9,280	58%	14.7%
Commons Maths	1,574	27,893	725	26,053	54%	6.6%	1,544	27,574	793	26,089	49%	5.4%
Ebean	811	9,565	363	8,182	55%	14.5%	799	9,450	377	8,424	53%	10.9%
Fauxpas	23	39	6	27	74%	30.7%	23	41	6	28	74%	31.7%
JSoup	240	2,660	127	2,394	47%	10.0%	233	2,656	131	2,436	44%	8.3%
Spoon	482	9,683	233	9,447	52%	2.4%	477	10,123	239	9,563	50%	5.5%

RQ4 – How much time can be saved per test run and are the time savings proportional to the number of omitted tests?

In Fig. 2 we give an overview of the time savings of the different algorithms applied to all of our study subjects. The y-axis shows the time savings in percent of the runtime of the full test suite. First, we can observe that the results vary a lot between the different projects. The time savings range from 4.5% to 68.6%. However, for most of our study subjects, the savings of all minimization techniques exceed 35%, making the benefits of test suite minimization quite attractive.

A, to us, surprising result is that the project with the smallest time savings, the Apache Commons Collections library, also has the highest relative reduction in its test suite size. This suggests that execution time of the test suites is not equally distributed. The removal of few, long running tests has more impact than omitting as many tests as possible. A good indicator for this is the difference between the inadequate versions of the algorithms for the Apache Commons Collections library and the adequate versions. The difference in the number of selected tests is rather small but the savings increase a lot more than they did with the first ~93% of removed tests.

Regarding the difference between the greedy and HGS algorithms, we can, once again, not determine a consistently superior algorithm. However, the inadequate versions of both algorithms show clear improvement over their adequate counterparts reaching from 4.4% to 24.3%.

By including the execution time of the individual test cases in the minimization, the variation in the effectiveness of test suite minimization could most likely be reduced considerably.

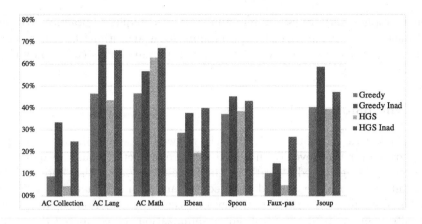

Fig. 2. Time Savings of Test Suite Minimization

7 Threats to Validity

In this section, to understand the limitations of our evaluation of test suite minimization, we discuss some possible threats that could affect the validity of our results.

Internal Threats. The first possible criticism of our method is the use of mutation testing as a replacement for real faults. Though, it has been shown that the ability of a test suite to kill mutants is highly correlated with its ability to detect real faults [1,2,4], mutants are not the same thing as real faults. Another problem of mutation testing are equivalent mutants which cannot be detected and endless loops which can be caused by mutants. However, since our results involve mainly comparisons of the loss of mutation score from test suite minimization, the overall mutation score is not critical for the validity of our results.

Another issue of mutation testing is that timeouts can vary between test runs. Since mutation testing can cause infinite loops, there is a timeout value necessary to keep the mutation testing going when an infinite loop has been created. However, this can also happen by accident if a test runs longer than it should for some reason. We found a variation in timeouts between runs caused by false positives in the determination of timeouts. However, the margin between our runs did not exceed 1% in our results.

External Threats. There is no guarantee that these results are representative beyond the scope of our study subjects. Even though, we used actively developed open source projects from different developers, commercial, closed source projects and other open source projects with very different characteristics may behave different with regard to test suite minimization. The projects we chose were limited in size due to the cost of mutation testing being fairly high and it's compatibility, especially with complicated builds being fairly low. Furthermore, we investigated only a small set of proposed minimization techniques to evaluate applicability of test suite minimization techniques in practice. We have implemented two common test suite minimization algorithms but there are a lot more, also incorporating different testing requirements instead of only using statement coverage.

8   Conclusion

We evaluated the benefits and drawbacks of two test suite minimization algorithms over a range of seven open source software projects. We used two different statement coverage-based algorithms, the basic greedy algorithm and the HGS algorithm. For both, we applied an adequate and an inadequate variant to all of our study subjects. To find out, how well the fault detection capability of a test suite is maintained after test suite minimization, we compared the results of mutation testing of the full test suites and the minimized ones. We found that with the algorithms we used, there is a considerable trade-off between the reduction in test suite size and the loss in fault detection capability. The number of test cases was reduced by at least 50% for all the study subjects; the average reduction of our adequate algorithms being around 69% of tests removed.

To get an insight into the practical benefits of test suite minimization, we measured the execution time of test suites of our study subjects before and after the test suites were minimized. We found that, even though there were substantial reductions in all projects, there is a huge range between the execution time reduction of the individual projects (5% to 69%). The reduction in number of tests appears to be a bad indicator for the reduction in execution time.

Overall, test suite minimization shows great potential in terms of test suite execution time reduction. However, the implementation we chose in this paper does not provide a great trade-off between runtime improvements and loss in fault detection.

9   Future Work

We found that using statement coverage as the only criterion for minimization, while producing great results in terms of test suite size, leads to a substantial loss in fault detection capability which, in practice, will not be acceptable in a lot of cases. That is why we plan on investigating multiple objective-based algorithms, which could improve the outcome of test suite minimization in terms of the maintained fault detection capability. Another factor in a multi objective approach could be execution time, which shows substantial reductions in our experiments but could most likely be improved by introducing it as a criterion to be optimized for.

Another interesting possibility, which we want to pursue, is be to increase the variety of study subjects by shifting the focus from only open source projects to include closed source projects as well. Covering as many different ways of software development as possible can increase the viability of test suite minimization. So far it is rarely used in practice. Proving that commercial projects can gain from test suite minimization could benefit its propagation from the domain of research into widespread use.

Future research could also evaluate test suite minimization techniques on the basis of real faults from the past according to how many of them are found. This would deliver even more relevant results than using mutation testing but finding and extracting data of sufficient volume for this kind of evaluation is much more difficult and laborious than using generated mutants.

References

1. Andrews, J.H., Briand, L.C., Labiche, Y.: Is mutation an appropriate tool for testing experiments? In: Proceedings of the 27th International Conference on Software Engineering, pp. 402–411. ACM (2005)
2. Andrews, J.H., Briand, L.C., Labiche, Y., Namin, A.S.: Using mutation analysis for assessing and comparing testing coverage criteria. IEEE Trans. Softw. Eng. **32**(8), 608–624 (2006)
3. Chen, T.Y., MF, L.: Dividing strategies for the optimization of a test suite. Inf. Process. Lett. **60**(3), 135–141 (1996)
4. Do, H., Rothermel, G.: On the use of mutation faults in empirical assessments of test case prioritization techniques. IEEE Trans. Softw. Eng. **32**(9), 733–752 (2006)
5. Harman, M.: Making the case for MORTO: multi objective regression test optimization. In: 2011 IEEE Fourth International Conference on Software Testing, Verification and Validation Workshops, pp. 111–114. IEEE (2011)
6. Harrold, M.J., Gupta, R., Soffa, M.L.: A methodology for controlling the size of a test suite. ACM Trans. Softw. Eng. Methodol. (TOSEM) **2**(3), 270–285 (1993)
7. Jeffrey, D., Gupta, N.: Test suite reduction with selective redundancy. In: 21st IEEE International Conference on Software Maintenance (ICSM 2005), pp. 549–558. IEEE (2005)
8. Jeffrey, D., Gupta, N.: Improving fault detection capability by selectively retaining test cases during test suite reduction. IEEE Trans. Softw. Eng. **33**(2), 108–123 (2007)
9. Jia, Y., Harman, M.: An analysis and survey of the development of mutation testing. IEEE Trans. Softw. Eng. **37**(5), 649–678 (2010)
10. Pan, J., Loudon Tech Center: Procedures for reducing the size of coverage-based test sets. In: Proceedings of International Conference on Testing Computer Software, pp. 111–123. Citeseer (1995)
11. Papadimitriou, C.H., Steiglitz, K.: Combinatorial Optimization: Algorithms and Complexity. Courier Corporation (1998)
12. Rothermel, G., Harrold, M.J., Ostrin, J., Hong, C.: An empirical study of the effects of minimization on the fault detection capabilities of test suites. In: Proceedings of the International Conference on Software Maintenance (Cat. No. 98CB36272), pp. 34–43. IEEE (1998)
13. Rothermel, G., Harrold, M.J., Von Ronne, J., Hong, C.: Empirical studies of test-suite reduction. Softw. Test. Verif. Reliab. **12**(4), 219–249 (2002)
14. Shi, A., Gyori, A., Gligoric, M., Zaytsev, A., Marinov, D.: Balancing trade-offs in test-suite reduction. In: Proceedings of the 22nd ACM SIGSOFT International Symposium on Foundations of Software Engineering, pp. 246–256. ACM (2014)
15. Tallam, S., Gupta, N.: A concept analysis inspired greedy algorithm for test suite minimization. ACM SIGSOFT Softw. Eng. Notes **31**(1), 35–42 (2006)

16. Wei, Z., Xiaoxue, W., Xibing, Y., Shichao, C., Wenxin, L., Jun, L.: Test suite minimization with mutation testing-based many-objective evolutionary optimization. In: 2017 International Conference on Software Analysis, Testing and Evolution (SATE), pp. 30–36. IEEE (2017)
17. Wong, W.E., Horgan, J.R., London, S., Mathur, A.P.: Effect of test set minimization on fault detection effectiveness. Softw. Pract. Exp. **28**(4), 347–369 (1998)
18. Wong, W.E., Horgan, J.R., Mathur, A.P., Pasquini, A.: Test set size minimization and fault detection effectiveness: a case study in a space application. In: Proceedings Twenty-First Annual International Computer Software and Applications Conference (COMPSAC 1997), pp. 522–528. IEEE (1997)
19. Yoo, S., Harman, M.: Regression testing minimization, selection and prioritization: a survey. Softw. Test. Verif. Reliab. **22**(2), 67–120 (2012)
20. Zhang, L., Marinov, D., Zhang, L., Khurshid, S.: An empirical study of JUnit test-suite reduction. In: 2011 IEEE 22nd International Symposium on Software Reliability Engineering, pp. 170–179. IEEE (2011)

Social Aspects in Software Engineering

Soft Competencies and Satisfaction Levels for Software Engineers: A Unified Framework

Nana Assyne[(✉)]

Faculty of Information Technology, University of Jyväskylä, Jyväskylä, Finland
nana.m.a.assyne@student.jyu.fi

Abstract. The importance of software engineers' competency has long been established as a key pillar for the development of robust software in order to achieve quality software. Software engineering competency research is not necessarily lacking. Nevertheless, the satisfaction derived from using software competency needs more investigation. The aim of this study is to identify soft competencies from empirical data and create satisfaction levels for software engineers' soft competencies. The result shows 63 soft competencies with three different satisfaction levels consisting of basic, performance and delighters. The paper contributes to the SEC research by highlighting the satisfaction levels of soft competency for the benefit of the educators (academia), software engineers (possessor) and users of software competency (practitioner).

Keywords: Soft competency · Software engineers' competencies · Competency satisfaction levels · Essential competencies

1 Introduction

The competencies of software engineers have long been recognized as essential for the development of efficient and robust software [1]. According to IEEE software engineering competency is defined as the knowledge, skills and attitudes of software developers to fulfill a task in a software development project [2]. This includes both soft and hard competencies [3]. Lenberg et al. pointed out that research work on software engineering competency (SEC) is not necessarily lacking. Yet, most of the earlier research on SEC focused on technical or hard competencies as against soft or behavioral competencies [4]. Harris & Rogers, define soft skills or competencies as "work ethics, positive attitude, social grace, facility with language, friendliness, integrity and the willingness to learn" [5, p.19]. Thus, the identification and use of soft competencies help in the development of complex software, because the software development involves a combination of soft and hard competencies [3, 6].

Works of authors such as Broadbent et al., Moreno et al., and Colomo-palacios et al. have established that soft competency is essential for development of software [6–8]. More importantly, recent literature suggests an increase in the number of software soft competencies studies with emphasis on identification of soft competencies [4]. Holtkamp et al. argued that, soft competencies are crucial for the development of global software

© Springer Nature Switzerland AG 2020
D. Winkler et al. (Eds.): SWQD 2020, LNBIP 371, pp. 69–83, 2020.
https://doi.org/10.1007/978-3-030-35510-4_5

engineering [9]. Nonetheless, the satisfaction levels of these competencies have not been adequately explored. Accordingly, this paper reports the identification and satisfaction levels of soft SEC as part of a bigger research on SEC.

The knowledge or identification of competencies is one phase of competency equation. The other phase is the benefit derived in the using such competency. The second phases have not received much attention in SEC research. Thurner et al. argue for minimum or base competency as a basic requirement for students of software engineering [10]. We support the base competency requirement and advocate for further investigations to determine the various levels of satisfaction of competencies. We therefore argue for satisfaction levels of soft competencies for software engineers, and state our research questions as:

RQ1: What are the different satisfaction levels derived from using a software soft competency?

RQ2: Which of these soft competencies are perceived as most valuable for Software engineering?

Knowledge of soft competencies and their satisfaction levels serve as insurance for users (people or organizations who use the competencies possessed by the developers to produce a product or a service), educator (people who train the developers to acquire the competencies), and the engineers' (people who receive training and therefore possesses some competencies). Therefore, we have adopt the Kano model [11] and Competency Framework for Software Engineers (CFSE) [12] as a lens to develop satisfaction rankings that can be employed by (i) the possessor of the competencies, (ii) users of the competencies and (iii) by the trainer of competencies possessors. The rest of the paper is presented as follows: Sect. 2 looks at the background and related works and discuss the research models; Sect. 3 discusses the methodology; Sect. 4 presents the results; and Sects. 5 and 6 looks at the discussions and conclusions respectively.

2 Theoretical Foundation and Related Works

2.1 Soft Competency

According to Harris & Rogers, soft skill is or are skills that mostly do not require formal training [5]. Until recently, these skills were mostly self-taught and self-developed. They are mostly not industry specific. In addition, they mostly require emotional intelligence [13, 14] e.g. communication flexibility, leadership, motivation, patience, persuasion, problem-solving abilities, teamwork, time management, work ethics.

Soft competency connotes skills that complement technical skills; therefore, it cannot be overlooked in the development of software engineering. [They complement technical skills and thus cannot be overlooked in software engineering]. They are considered to be essential for global software projects [9, p.136]. (Broadbent et al. established that the biggest skill gaps for software engineers were business strategies and marketing of their services [7]. This was emphasized by Moreno et al. [6]. Other studies have argued that more attention must be given to social and inter-personal competencies [15] and emotional intelligence [16].

In proposing a body of skills (SWEBOS) for software engineering, Sedelmaier and Landes identified and structured soft competencies of software engineers into three categories [3]. These include (i) comprehension of the complexity of software engineering processes, (ii) awareness of problems and understanding of cause-effect relationships, and (iii) team competency including communication skills. Although, this provided useful information that facilitates software development practices, it fails to provide relevant information regarding the satisfaction levels derived for possessing or using a competency. Evidently, there is a gap in existing literature. Perhaps, this is because researchers in the area of behavioral of software engineering have been focusing on few concepts [4] and ignore other relevant issues such as the assurance for using or possessing a particular competency.

To address this, this study seeks to identify and also create a satisfaction level of the competencies from perspective of users, educators, and engineers. This will complement research on SEC in general and soft competency research specifically. To enable us to achieve our research objectives, we make use of CFSE and Kano model. The next sub-sections discuss CFSE and the Kano model.

2.2 Kano Model

The Kano model is a quality function-deployment framework that helps developers of product or service to include customer's voice in the development phase. It has been applied mostly in the development of products. This is because it takes into consideration the views of both the customer and developer in the development of a product instead of a passive approach of only developers [17, 17–23] used the Kano model for the development of ICT system and concluded that the model prioritizes user involvement. It assists in determining basic, performance and delighters of a product or service.

In our scenario, the customer is the software community (organization using the competencies) and the product or service is the competency. According to Kano et al. customer's decision-making options on product or service acquisition, are based on conscious and subconscious deliberations [11]. There is therefore the need to understand these deliberative conscious and subconscious processes of decision-making to help develop products or services. Kano et al. categorized these processes into three-requirement levels (basic, performance and delighters). Basic requirements relate to customer's expectations about a product or service. These requirements are classified as basic since their presence are not dynamic enough to change the options and opinion a customer has about the product. However, their absence may result in complaints from the customer. Performance requirements, on the other hand, are expected pre-requisites that customers know and they are essential influential factors on the customer's decision-making options on products or services. These are critical pre-requisite requirements that create high levels of satisfaction when employed appropriately and otherwise if not used. The last requirement termed delighters are those requirements that do not engender any complaints from the customers when absent however surprises the customer when present. Delighters are sometimes referred to as attractive or "wow" factors [11].

2.3 Competency Framework for Software Engineers

Competency Framework for Software Engineers (CFSE) is a framework that facilitates, identifies the training needs, and guides the design of software engineers' competencies. The design is based on the activities and interactions of engineers during the software development process. The constructs of this framework are under the main classification of competency (Hard and Soft). Hard competency category relates to the technical aspects of software engineering. These aspects are based on the definition of the SWE-BOK roles in software engineering. They are project management, requirement analysis, software design, programming, validation and verification tests, configuration management, quality, tests, documentation and maintenance. The soft part of the categorization is classified into social and personal. Social aspects include interpersonal relations, cooperation and work in a team, and handling and conflicts resolution. Personals on the other hand includes development in the job, personal development, rights and limits. It can broadly be considered as "a set of knowledge, abilities and key behaviors, with special emphasis on the soft skills" [12].

The objective is to create a classificatory system that identifies and explains satisfaction levels of software engineers' competencies. Therefore, we consider the framework suitable. This is because it considers both soft and hard competency and this is the bigger objective we intend to achieve. Furthermore, the framework considers granularity, which is essential for fitting the work to the community. In line with the objective of this study, we focus on the soft competency aspect of the framework and merge it with Kano model. This resulted in a unified framework for identifying and classifying the satisfaction levels of soft competencies. For detailed analysis of the individual meanings of critical variables of CFSE, readers can refer to the original paper of [12]. The detail of the proposed framework for this paper is explained in the next section.

3 A Unified Framework of Soft Competency Satisfaction Levels for Software Engineers (UFSCSL)

As mentioned earlier, the framework is derived from the CFSE and Kano model. From the CFSE we made use of the soft competency category since our aim is to identify and classify only the soft competency. From among frameworks such as [24–27] for identifying software engineering competencies CFSE framework is the one that has more granularity, thus making it easy for in-depth analysis. In addition, the Kano model has been used for research work in software engineering, but not for analyzing competencies. Thus, this provides a means to chart a new path for competency research. The soft part of the CFSE framework is first categorized into socials and personals and each have lower granularity as shown in Fig. 1. The variables of the Kano model (basic, performance, and delighters) were included, to provide the satisfaction levels for the competencies. See Fig. 1 for the "soft satisfaction levels of software engineers" framework.

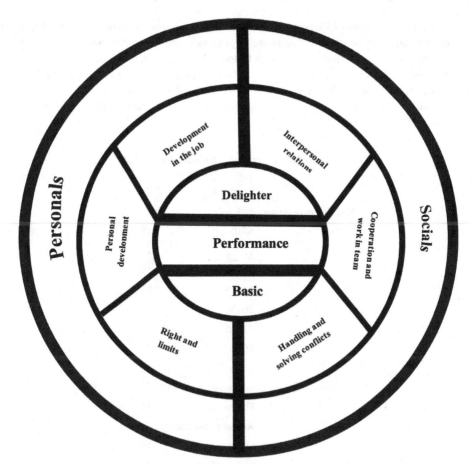

Fig. 1. Unified framework of soft competency satisfaction levels for software engineers (UFSCSL)

To use the UFSCSL, first, the competencies are identified and classifying using the variables in [12] within the frameworks. Then each competency identified or classified is subjected to the metrics of Kano model (see Sect. 2.2) to determines its satisfaction levels. Thus, given as basic, performance and delighter competencies for socials (interpersonal relations, cooperation and work in a team, and handling and conflicts resolution) and personals (development in the job, personal development, rights and limits).

4 Methodology

4.1 Data Collection

An exploratory qualitative study was adopted. Specifically, [28, 29] qualitative research guide was employed to extrapolate the required data. We agree with the philosophy that an individual's behavior is influenced by the meanings attached to events [30]. Thus, one hundred and thirty-eight (138) participants were drawn from workers in various positions within the industry: practitioner/software engineers/managers/supervisors/mentor. All participants were from software industries based in Norway. A semi-structured interview was used for data collection. Interviews were face-to-face and focused on expected skills of a software developer. Each interview session lasted for about 1 h. The interview was conducted with the support of assistants. Table 1 represents the distribution of respondents' characteristics.

Table 1. Respondents characteristics

	Category	Freq
Years of experience	1–5	40
	6–10	17
	11–15	7
	16–20	15
	21–25	11
	26–30	13
	31–35	2
	36–40	2
	unspecified	31
Background	Software	72
	Hardware	11
	Research/university	11
	Others	19
	Unspecified	25

4.2 Data Analysis

A thematic analysis offers an accessible means for organizing and describing a dataset under specific themes. Currently, there is no widely agreed way of going about how to use the method [31]. The soft competency satisfaction framework was therefore adopted to guide the analysis.

Both inductive analysis and deductive analysis were used. The coding of the data was done without any pre-defined framework. This enable the themes to emerge from the data. The framework (UFSCSL) was then applied to further code the theme that emerged from the data. Two categories were used on the bases of the epistemology of this research. That is, we were aware of the competencies that have been identified and exist in literature, but our epistemology was that within those identified there will be different satisfaction levels. Hence, we employed both categories in this paper. We outline the following steps below based on the outcome of our analysis and guided by the steps of [31].

Step 1 Familiarization of the Data
The interview was conducted with the help of assistants, with the aim of capturing large groups of respondents. Each interviewer transcribed his or her own interview. The author of this paper acquainted himself by reading through the transcribed scripts. During this stage, notes were taken in cases where there were difficulties in understanding aspects of the data. Further discussions were made with the head of data collection to resolve any ambiguity in the data.

Step 2 Generating Initial Codes
Initial codes were generated from the data by extracting keywords. This was done without recourse to initial pre-defined coding framework. The total number of competencies that were identified from the transcribed data were six hundred forty-one.

Step 3 Searching for Themes
After the initial code, all initial codes were grouped into themes, this facilitated the identification of themes. These themes were generated without resort to pre-defined coding framework. Three hundred sixty soft competencies were identified at this stage.

Step 4 Reviewing Themes
The themes were compared with existing themes. That is, a pre-defining coding framework was also used. In this case, the Rivera-Ibarra et al. [12] CFSE framework was used.

Step 5 Defining and Naming
Next defined themes and meanings were assigned. These names and meanings were reviewed with literature before the competencies were validated using the variables in the Kano model. This stage resulted in 22 basics, 26 performance and 16 delighter competencies.

Phase 6 Producing the Report
The emerged themes that resulted from comparing data themes and themes from the framework were used to produce the results discussed in the next section.

5 Results

5.1 RQ1: What Are the Different Satisfaction Levels Derived from Using a Software Soft Competency?

We present the result in Table 2 using the framework (UFSCSL) developed for this paper. The results show the individual competencies and their satisfaction levels, that is: basic, performance, and delighters. They were grouped according to the broader theme of soft competency: social and personal. We also provided definitions using the classification levels from the Kano model for the competencies.

Basic
From the interview data and the analysis, basic competencies are pre-requisite competencies that are necessary and are expected by the users of the competency. Mostly they

Table 2. Soft competencies and their satisfaction Levels

	Satisfaction levels	Software engineer competencies
Socials		
Interpersonal relations	Delight	(i) communicate to outside world, and (ii) sociable
	Performance	(i) communication skill, (ii) adaptability, (iii) human skill, and (iv) interpersonal skill
	Basic	(i) social skills and (ii) contributing to the society
Cooperation and work in team	Delight	(i) Excellent teacher, (ii) see bigger picture, and (iii) leadership
	Performance	(i) team work, (ii) team organizer, (iii) approachable, (iv) open and communicating, (v) learn from others, and (vi) voice your own opinions
	Basic	(i) Cooperation, (ii) maturity, (iii) teach and share knowledge, and (iv) dedication to work
Handling and solving conflicts	Delight	(i) humbleness, (ii) customer awareness, and (iii) understand customer needs
	Performance	(i) meeting skills, and (ii) contact with clients
	Basic	(i) Listen ears, (ii) compromise, and (iii) empathy
Personals		
Development in the job environment	Delight	(i) unafraid, (ii) creative and brave, and (iii) think outside the box
	Performance	(i) persistence, (ii) flexible, (iii) versatile, (iv) focus, (v) accuracy, (vi) analytical skills, (vii) logical mindset and keep and overview, and (viii) creativity
	Basic	(i) Willingness to learn, (ii) curious, (iii) passionate about your job, (iv) ask questions, (v) confidence, (vi) honest and responsible
Personal development	Delight	(i) can apply theories in application, (ii) see opportunity in systems, (iii) initiative, (iv) separate work and being available, and (v) self-sufficient
	Performance	(i) precise and detail oriented, (ii) self-reliance, (ii) independence (iv) understand needs for further development, and (v) know the working environments
	Basic	(ii) pragmatic, (iii) patience, and (iii) open to new ideas
Right and limits	Delight	–
	Performance	(i) attention to detail
	Basic	(i) Introspection and admit error, (ii) admit ignorance, and (iii) interest in the field

are taken for granted. Users see these competencies as natural when delivered properly. However, when delivered poorly, users will complain.

Performance

From the interview data and the analysis performance competencies are what users expect and can articulate. They are mostly in the minds of the users and when they are delivered well, they create more satisfaction. These competencies can be described as "uni-dimensional" competency, in that the satisfaction grows exponentially when executed properly.

Delighters

From the interview data and the analysis, the delighter competencies are unexpected by the user. Mostly unexpected by the user but increases the delight and surprise when available however its absence may have no effect on user.

5.2 RQ2: Which of These Soft Competencies Are Perceived as Most Valuable for Software Engineering?

As mentioned earlier, delighters are attractive or wow factors that valuable for the development of a product [11]. Therefore, we present our delighter competencies as the most

Table 3. Most valuable competencies.

Competency area	Competency name
Socials	
Interpersonal relations	Communicate to outside world
	Sociable
Cooperation and work in team	Excellent teacher
	See bigger picture
	Leadership
Personals	
Handling and solving conflicts	Humbleness
	Customer awareness
	Understand customer needs
Development in the job environment	Unafraid
	Creative and brave
	Think outside the box
Personal development	Can applied theories in application
	See opportunity in systems
	Initiative
	Separate work and being available
	Self-sufficient

Table 4. Total number of soft competencies based on the satisfaction levels classification

Competency area	Satisfaction levels		Total number
Socials			
Interpersonal relations	Delight	2	8
	Performance	4	
	Basic	2	
Cooperation and work in team	Delight	3	13
	Performance	6	
	Basic	4	
Handling and solving conflicts	Delight	3	8
	Performance	2	
	Basic	3	
Personals			
Development in the job environment	Delight	3	17
	Performance	8	
	Basic	6	
Personal development	Delight	5	13
	Performance	5	
	Basic	3	
Right and limits	Delight	0	4
	Performance	1	
	Basic	3	
Total			

valuable or essential competencies for software engineering. The Table 3 shows the competency based on Rivera-Ibarra et al. CFSE framework [12]. The table shows the competency category and the identified essential soft competency for software engineers that are useful for software development.

6 Discussions

Following our analysis, we aimed to provide a satisfaction level for the competencies identified from our primary data. A total of 63 competencies emerge from our data. Out of that 29 was for social competencies and 34 was for personals competencies with three satisfaction levels.

Table 4 shows the number of competencies and number of satisfactions of the competency area. Under socials competency area cooperation and work in team had 13 competencies, interpersonal relations and handling and solving conflicts had 8 competencies each. The cooperation and work in team competency reflect the team competency

Table 5. Identified soft competencies and prior work.

Category	Identified soft competency	Comparison
Socials		
Interpersonal relations	Sociable, communication skill, adaptability, human skill, interpersonal skill, social skills	Consistent with prior work
	Communicate to outside world, contributing to the society,	New observations
Cooperation and work in team	See bigger picture, leadership, team work, Cooperation, teach and share knowledge, team organizer, approachable, open and communicating, learn from others	Consistent with prior work
	Maturity, Excellent teacher, voice your own opinions. dedication to work	New observations
Handling and solving conflicts	Customer awareness, understand customer needs, meeting skills, contact with clients, empathy	Consistent with prior work
	Humbleness, compromise	New observations
Personals		
Development in the job environment	Unafraid, creative and brave, think outside the box, persistence, flexible, versatile, analytical skills, creativity, Willingness to learn, curious, ask questions, confidence, focus, accuracy, logical mindset and keep and overview, honest and responsible	Consistent with prior work
	Passionate about your job	New observations
Personal development	Separate work and being available, self-sufficient, precise and detail oriented, self-reliance, independence, pragmatic, patience, initiative, open to new ideas	Consistent with prior work
	Can apply theories in application, see opportunity in systems, understand needs for further development, know the working environments	New observations
Right and limits	Attention to detail,	Consistent with prior work
	Introspection and admit error, admit ignorance, interest in the field	New observations

category of Sedelmaier and Landes [3]. Under personals competency area, development in the job environment had 17 competencies, followed by personal development with 13 and right and limits with 4 competencies.

Some of the identified competencies in the categories are consistent with exiting literature such as the work of [3, 15, 16, 32–34]. Table 5 highlights the new observations and comparison to prior work. With regard to satisfaction levels, competencies were identified in all the categories except rights and limits delighters. A total of 16 essential competencies using the Kano model was identified. These competencies are consistent with literatures such as [35, 36]. Furthermore we have been able to create a satisfaction level, that adds to the works of [10, 37] that made argument for based competencies.

On the essential soft competencies for software engineers, we have been able use model analysis to extrapolate the essential competencies that are in agreements with the work of [35, 36, 38]. Thus, providing a new way of identifying essential competencies.

The novelty in this work are: (i) observations of new soft competency from empirical data that are highlighted in Table 4 and (ii) the Unified framework of soft competency satisfaction levels for software engineers (UFSCSL). The UFSCSL has the ability to identify soft competencies of software engineers and also provide a satisfaction levels of the competency. Thus, serving as insurance model for users, possessors and the educators. In short, the major stakeholders of software engineering competency development are considered in this framework.

The study has both practical and research implications. From the perspective of the users of competencies, they can use the classification to determine which competencies will be valuable for employment. On the part of the possessor, they can use the classification levels to evaluate what they possess. Furthermore, educators can use the classification levels to adjust their training. Additionally, the framework which was proposed (UFSCSL) can be used for constant evaluation on old competencies and also on new ones.

7 Conclusion

The study has analyzed, identified and created a classification that can be used by the software community. This was done by synthesized existing relevant literature. The empirical work was based on Kano et al. [11] and Rivera-Ibarra et al. [12] CFSE framework. The study resulted in the identification of competencies, classification levels and essential competencies of software engineers. The study charts a new path of identifying essential or valued competencies of software engineers by using Kano model that has on been applied on products and services. Further studies should be done to understand how competencies within the satisfaction level can change.

The scope of the data collection was limited to companies situated in Norway; it may therefore limit the ability to generalize the findings universally. Nevertheless, most of the companies that the interviewees worked for has global representation and dealings outside Norway. With the development of competency satisfaction levels, we call for further studies to understand how specific competencies evolves within the satisfaction level.

Acknowledgement. The author would like to acknowledge Prof. Pekka Abrahamsson for his support in providing the dataset for this research and Dr. Hadi Ghanbari for his guidance.

References

1. Weinberg, G.M.: The Psychology of Computer Programming. Dorset House Publishing, New York (1971)
2. IEEE: Software Engineering Competency Model (SWECOM). IEEE. (2014). http://www.dahlan.web.id/files/ebooks/SWECOM.pdf
3. Sedelmaier, Y., Landes, D.: Software engineering body of skills (SWEBOS). In: 2014 IEEE Global Engineering Education Conference (EDUCON), pp. 395–401. IEEE (2014). https://doi.org/10.1109/educon.2014.6826125
4. Lenberg, P., Feldt, R., Wallgren, L.G.: Behavioral software engineering: A definition and systematic literature review. J. Syst. Softw. **107**, 15–37 (2015). https://doi.org/10.1016/j.jss.2015.04.084
5. Harris, K.S., Rogers, G.E.: Soft skills in the technology education classroom: what do students need. Technol. Teacher **68**(3), 19–25 (2008)
6. Moreno, A.M., Sanchez-segura, M., Medina-dominguez, F., Carvajal, L.: The journal of systems and software balancing software engineering education and industrial needs. J. Syst. Softw. **85**(7), 1607–1620 (2012). https://doi.org/10.1016/j.jss.2012.01.060
7. Broadbent, M., Dampney, C.N.G., Lloyd, P., Hansell, A.: Roles, responsibilities and requirements for managing information systems in the 1990s. Int. J. Inf. Manage. **72**, 21–38 (1992)
8. Colomo-palacios, R., Casado-lumbreras, C., Soto-acosta, P., García-peñalvo, F.J., Tovar-caro, E.: Computers in human behavior competence gaps in software personnel: a multi-organizational study. Comput. Hum. Behav. **29**(2), 456–461 (2013). https://doi.org/10.1016/j.chb.2012.04.021
9. Holtkamp, P., Jokinen, J.P.P., Pawlowski, J.M.: Soft competency requirements in requirements engineering, software design, implementation, and testing. J. Syst. Softw. **101**, 136–146 (2015). https://doi.org/10.1016/j.jss.2014.12.010
10. Thurner, V., Schlierkamp, K., Bottcher, A., Zehetmeier, D.: Integrated development of technical and base competencies: fostering reflection skills in software engineers to be. In: IEEE Global Engineering Education Conference, EDUCON, pp. 340–348. Abu Dhabi, UAE: IEEE (2016). https://doi.org/10.1109/educon.2016.7474576
11. Kano, N., Seraku, N., Takahashi, F., Tsuji, S.: Kano. attractive quality and must-be quality. J. Japanese Soc. Qual. Control **14**, 39–48 (1984)
12. Rivera-Ibarra, J.G., Rodríguez-Jacobo, J., Serrano-Vargas, M.A.: Competency framework for software engineers. In: 2010 23rd IEEE Conference on Software Engineering Education and Training, pp. 33–40 (2010). https://doi.org/10.1109/cseet.2010.21
13. Andrews, J., Higson, H.: Graduate employability, 'soft skills' versus 'hard' business knowledge: a european study. Higher Educ. Eur. **33**(4), 411–422 (2008). https://doi.org/10.1080/03797720802522627
14. Trivellas, P., Reklitis, P.: Leadership Competencies Profiles and Managerial Effectiveness in Greece. In: Procedia Economics and Finance, 9(Ebeec 2013), pp. 380–390 (2014). https://doi.org/10.1016/s2212-5671(14)00039-2
15. Licorish, S.A., Macdonell, S.G.: Differences in jazz project leaders' competencies and behaviors : a preliminary empirical investigation. In: 2013 6th International Workshop on Cooperative and Human Aspects of Software Engineering (CHASE), pp. 1–8. IEEE (2013). https://doi.org/10.1109/chase.2013.6614725
16. Noorman, M., Akmal, M., Osman, F., Ibrahim, Z.: Malaysian computer professional : assessment of emotional intelligence and organizational commitment. In: Procedia - Social and Behavioral Sciences, vol. 172, pp. 238–245. Elsevier B.V. (2015). https://doi.org/10.1016/j.sbspro.2015.01.360

17. Lee, Y.C., Sheu, L.C., Tsou, Y.G.: Quality function deployment implementation based on fuzzy kano model: an application in PLM system. Comput. Ind. Eng. **55**(1), 48–63 (2008). https://doi.org/10.1016/j.cie.2007.11.014

18. Gangurde, S., Patil, S.: Benchmark product features using the Kano-QFD approach: a case study. Benchmarking: an Int. J. **25**(2), 450–470 (2018)

19. Huang, J. (2018). Application of Kano model and IPA on improvement of service quality of mobile healthcare Jui-Chen Huang, 16(2)

20. Lehtola, L., Kauppinen, M.: Suitability of requirements prioritization methods for market-driven software product development. Softw. Process Improv. Pract. **11**(1), 7–19 (2006). https://doi.org/10.1002/spip.249

21. Liu, X.F.: Software quality function deployment. Potentials, IEEE **19**(5), 14–16 (2000). https://doi.org/10.1109/45.890072

22. Piaszczyk, C.: Model based systems engineering with department of defense architectural framework. Syst. Eng. **14**(3), 305–326 (2011). https://doi.org/10.1002/sys

23. Richardson, I.: Software process matrix: a small company SPI model. Software Process: Improvement and Practice, 6(Daft 1992), 157–165 (2001). https://doi.org/10.1002/spip.144

24. Orsoni, A., Colaco, B.: A competency framework for software development organizations. In: 2013 UKSim 15th International Conference on Computer Modelling and Simulation, pp. 507–511). IEEE (2013). https://doi.org/10.1109/uksim.2013.101

25. Acuña, S.T., Juristo, N.: Assigning people to roles in software projects. Softw. – Pract. Exp. **34**(7), 675–696 (2004). https://doi.org/10.1002/spe.586

26. Linck, B., Ohrndorf, L., Kiel, T.D.L., Magenheim, J., Neugebauer, J.: Competence model for informatics modelling and system comprehension. In: 2013 IEEE Global Engineering Education Conference (EDUCON), pp. 85–93. IEEE (2013). https://doi.org/10.1109/educon.2013.6530090

27. Tuffley, D. Optimising virtual team leadership in Global Software Development. IET Software, 6(March 2011), pp. 176–184 (2012). https://doi.org/10.1049/iet-sen.2011.0044

28. Mason, J.: Qualitative Researching. Qualitative Research Journal, vol. 41 (2002). https://doi.org/10.1159/000105503

29. Myers, M.D., Newman, M.: The qualitative interview in IS research: Examining the craft. Inf. Organ. **17**(1), 2–26 (2007). https://doi.org/10.1016/j.infoandorg.2006.11.001

30. Wohlin, C., Aurum, A.: Towards a decision-making structure for selecting a research design in empirical software engineering. Empirical Softw. Eng. **20**(6), 1427–1455 (2015). https://doi.org/10.1007/s10664-014-9319-7

31. Braun, V., Clarke, V.: Full-text. Qual. Res. Psychol. **3**(2), 77–101 (2006). https://doi.org/10.1191/1478088706qp063oa

32. Kropp, M., Meier, A., Perellano, G.: Experience report of teaching agile collaboration and values agile software development in large student teams. In: 2016 IEEE 29th International Conference on Software Engineering Education and Training (CSEET), pp. 76–80. IEEE (2016). https://doi.org/10.1109/cseet.2016.30

33. Robal, T., Ojastu, D., Kalja, A., Jaakkola, H.: Managing software engineering competences with domain ontology for customer and team profiling and training. In: Portland International Conference on Management of 2015 Portland International Conference on Management of Engineering and Technology (PICMET), pp. 1369–1376 (2015). https://doi.org/10.1109/picmet.2015.7273171

34. Samuelsen, T., Colomo-palacios, R., Kristiansen, M.: Learning software project management in teams with diverse backgrounds. In: Fourth International Conference on Technological Ecosystems for Enhancing Multiculturality–TEEM 16 (2016)

35. Turley, T., Bieman, M.: Competencies nonexceptional of exceptional and software engineers. J. Syst. Softw. **28**(28), 19–38 (1995)

36. Chang, J., Wang, T., Lee, M.: Impacts of using creative thinking skills and open data on programming design in a computer-supported collaborative learning environment. In: 2016 IEEE 16th International Conference on Advanced Learning Technologies, pp. 396–400 (2016). https://doi.org/10.1109/icalt.2016.78
37. Thurner, V., Axel, B., Andreas, K.: Identifying base competencies as prerequisites for software engineering education. In IEEE Global Engineering Education Conference (EDUCON), pp. 1069–1076 (2014). https://doi.org/10.1109/educon.2014.6826240
38. Suhartono, J., Sudirwan, J., Background, A.: Academic competence of computer science graduate degree from the employer's perspective. In: 2016 International Conference on Information Management and Technology (ICIMTech), pp. 176–181. IEEE (2016). https://doi.org/10.1109/icimtech.2016.7930325

Natural Language Processing

Semantic Similarities in Natural Language Requirements

Henning Femmer[(✉)], Axel Müller, and Sebastian Eder

Qualicen GmbH, Lichtenbergstr. 8, 85748 Garching, Germany
{henning.femmer,axel.muller,sebastian.eder}@qualicen.de

Abstract. Semantic similarity information supports requirements tracing and helps to reveal important requirements quality defects such as redundancies and inconsistencies.

Previous work has applied semantic similarity algorithms to requirements, however, we do not know enough about the performance of machine learning and deep learning models in that context.

Therefore, in this work we create the largest dataset for analyzing the similarity of requirements so far through the use of Amazon Mechanical Turk, a crowd-sourcing marketplace for micro-tasks. Based on this dataset, we investigate and compare different types of algorithms for estimating semantic similarities of requirements, covering both relatively simple bag-of-words and machine learning models.

In our experiments, a model which relies on averaging trained word and character embeddings as well as an approach based on character sequence occurrences and overlaps achieve the best performances on our requirements dataset.

Keywords: Requirements engineering · Similarity detection · Machine learning

1 Introduction

Since a requirements specification defines the outcome of a particular product development process, it is necessary that the contained requirements fulfill important *quality factors* [1,2]. This is important because requirements are worthless if they are, for instance, not understandable or the defined set of requirements is not complete. In that case, the developers or manufacturers could misunderstand the desired characteristics and thus create a product that diverges from the expected result. Therefore, the quality of the requirements specification needs to be assured which is typically accomplished by inspecting and validating the created requirements with respect to different quality characteristics. Accordingly, requirements can have different *defects* if they do not satisfy these characteristics [3,4].

Several of these characteristics are related to the semantic similarity of requirements. For example, semantic similarity information would help to identify redundant requirements which impair the maintainability of a requirements

© Springer Nature Switzerland AG 2020
D. Winkler et al. (Eds.): SWQD 2020, LNBIP 371, pp. 87–105, 2020.
https://doi.org/10.1007/978-3-030-35510-4_6

document since changes would have to be carried out for all duplicate items. Furthermore, automatic similarity estimations could help revealing inconsistencies within the specification by helping to track similar requirements which might turn out to be contradictory regarding particular details. Besides that, the process of requirements tracing could be supported by automatically suggesting links between similar project artifacts like requirements, test cases or designs. By generating these traces in a faster and easier way due to automatic similarity analyses, requirements engineers would be supported in understanding the relationships between different artifacts and can thus better detect duplicates, inconsistencies or missing items. When extending this idea to specifications of different projects, the information about the similarity of their artifacts may reveal reusable components of prior projects thus helping to reduce project effort.

Therefore, having information about the semantic similarities of requirements could help to support requirements engineers or analysts during the requirements review [5].

As we discuss in Sect. 2, previous works looking into this topic focused mostly on information retrieval approaches. However, modern advances in machine learning, e.g. Alpha Go [6] give us a glimpse of the potential of machine learning. Each year, the most promising approaches for similarity detection are discussed in the SemEval community. In this work, we want to test their knowledge in the domain of requirements engineering.

1.1 Contribution of This Work

This paper provides a novel analysis of the performance of a variety of similarity detection algorithms, including both baseline information retrieval algorithms, but also machine learning based approaches, on a large dataset of 1000 pairs of natural language requirements.

1.2 Structure of This Work

In Sect. 2, we describe related work with respect to both requirements-independent semantic similarity algorithms as well as already applied similarity approaches within the domain of requirements engineering. In Sect. 3, we explain the required background knowledge to understand the content of this paper in particular regarding our applied semantic similarity algorithms. The design of our experiment which is intended to evaluate the different algorithms on a requirements dataset is portrayed in Sect. 4. We present and analyze the results of this experiment in Sect. 5. Based on these results, we conclude and come up with several interpretations which are discussed in Sect. 6. Finally, in Sect. 7, we summarize the content and gathered insights of this work.

2   Related Work

Our related work can be divided into semantic similarity approaches using general text data and approaches only focusing on requirements data.

2.1   Semantic Similarity Estimation of General Texts

The approach and study of our paper draws on the Natural Language Processing task of Semantic Textual Similarity introduced by Agirre et al. For this task, algorithms try to estimate the grade of semantic similarity between given sentence pairs [7]. However, models that have been proposed for this task have not been investigated in the context of requirements engineering yet.

Several introduced semantic similarity models use machine learning techniques with manually designed and engineered features. These features often rely on string-based lexical information such as word and character overlaps, on knowledge-based semantic word relations based on lexical-semantic resources like WordNet, on corpus-based vector space models like Latent Semantic Analysis, or on syntactic similarities and dependencies [7,8].

Other researchers have proposed artificial intelligence models that are capable of capturing semantic differences of sentences based on word order or sentence structures [9]. Such algorithms can, for example, use sentence vectors provided by models such as Nie and Bansal's sentence encoder [10], employ interaction modules for computing word and phrase relationships of sentences like in Parikh et al.'s model [11] or apply combinations of such components such as the neural network model proposed by He and Lin [12].

2.2   Semantic Similarity Estimation for Requirements

Several semantic similarity approaches have specifically been proposed for the domain of requirements engineering and often utilize lexical similarity measures.

Mihany et al. introduced a system for identifying reusable projects and components by the similarity of their requirements which was calculated based on word overlaps [13,14].

Natt och Dag et al. compared different lexical similarity measures for identifying equivalent requirements [5]. They further refined these approaches in order to map customer wishes to product requirements which relate to the same functional requirements. For that, they constructed and compared sentence vectors based on word occurrences and frequency weights [15,16].

Hayes et al. compared several similarity methods for the requirements tracing process in order to automatically identify potential links between similar artifacts. They experimented with term frequencies and weights (TF-IDF), Latent Semantic Indexing (LSI), incorporating thesaurus information as well as relevance feedback analysis. Thereby, artifacts were represented by word occurrence vectors [17]. Eder et al. also applied LSI for automatic requirements tracing intending to automate the determination of LSI configurations [18].

Mezghani et al. proposed a k-means clustering algorithm for detecting redundancies and inconsistencies in requirements. They applied their algorithm on combinations of given requirements and their extracted business terms using the Euclidean distance as a similarity metric [19].

Juergens et al. investigated clone detection for requirements specifications. Their approach tried to identify duplicates by analyzing suffix trees which were constructed based on the word sequences of requirements [20].

Falessi et al. experimented with different NLP techniques regarding the identification of equivalent requirements. Their applied approaches comprised combinations of algebraic models, term extraction techniques, weighting schemes and similarity metrics. Falessi et al. reported a bag-of-words approach as the best single NLP technique, however, they pointed out that a combination of different NLP techniques outperformed all available individual approaches [21].

2.3   Research Gap

Researchers on semantic textual similarity tasks have proposed different state-of-the-art machine learning approaches that have shown to outperform simpler information retrieval methods on general text data. Nevertheless, it has never been investigated whether such approaches can also yield superior performances when applied to requirements data.

3   Background

For this work, two concepts are relevant. First, we need to define similarity. Second, we need to define the algorithms that we want to apply.

3.1   Semantic Similarity

For the definition of semantic similarity within this work, we utilize an ordinal similarity scale with six different values. This scale has been introduced by Agirre et al. for the SemEval research workshops on semantic textual similarity and have been successfully applied in this linguistic community since 7 years (details e.g. in [22]).

The applied semantic similarity scale is shown in Table 1. As can be seen, the different levels reach from total dissimilarity in meaning to complete meaning equivalence. The intermediate similarity grades represent various degrees of partial similarity and meaning overlap [7], for example, considering the topics and details of given texts.

Table 1. Ordinal semantic similarity scale

Score	Explanation
0	The two sentences are completely dissimilar
1	The two sentences are not equivalent, but are on the same topic
2	The two sentences are not equivalent, but share some details
3	The two sentences are roughly equivalent, but some important information differs/is missing
4	The two sentences are mostly equivalent, but some unimportant details differ
5	The two sentences are completely equivalent, as they mean the same thing

3.2 Applied Algorithms

In this work, we compare the algorithms listed in Table 2. The selection is based on the most common and successful algorithms from the SemEval community [7], since these are obviously the most promising approaches. We cannot explain all used algorithms in detail. For a deeper introduction into this, please refer to the respective original works. The selected algorithms listed in Table 2 vary between *baselines*, *pre-trained*, *self-trained*, and *non-trained* approaches:

Baseline approaches are very simplistic approaches, e.g. counting tokens, that help to reflect on the complexity of the problem and the actual advantage of more sophisticated and complex approaches. **Pre-Trained** approaches came with already trained machine learning models provided by the original authors. **Self-Trained** approaches are machine learning algorithms that we trained ourselves using data that has been published for the SemEval workshops. **Non-Trained** approaches do not require training for applications.

4 Study Design

In this chapter, we describe the structure and setup of our study which we use to compare the performances of different semantic similarity algorithms on requirements data. The description and design of our study correspond to the experiment process as introduced by Wohlin et al. [32].

According to the *Goal Question Metric* approach of Basili et al. [33], we first define the goal of our study as well as related research questions that we will investigate and answer based on the obtained results measured by appropriate metrics. Afterwards, we describe the context and setup of our study including selected subjects, objects and instruments.

4.1 Goal Definition

To understand the overall setting and intention of our experiment, we first define the goal of this study:

Table 2. The different algorithms used in this study grouped into *baseline approaches*, as well as *pre-trained, self-trained*, and *non-trained* approaches, each in alphabetical order.

Algorithm	Description
Char ngram BOW	A baseline token-occurrence-based model incorporating both character trigrams and fourgrams as features into the sentence vectors whereby the corresponding vector values represent binary occurrence indicators of these tokens
Word2vec CBOW	As a baseline, Word2vec continuous bag of words (CBOW) is a widely used word embeddings approach
BiLSTM Avg	A pre-trained sentence encoder by Wieting et al. that uses a bi-directional LSTM and concatenates the hidden states of the forward and backward LSTM [23,24]
Charagram	A pre-trained sentence encoder by [25] based on character n-gram embeddings which are added together in order to retrieve sentence vectors
InferSent	A pre-trained sentence encoder model that is a bi-directional LSTM trained on Natural Language Inference data [26]
USE	As a pre-trained sentence encoder, Universal Sentence Encoders (USE) is an approach focussing on task and context generalizability [27]
Word-trigram	This pre-trained sentence encoder combines word and character trigram embeddings by averaging all embeddings for the character sequences and words contained in the given sentence, which outperformed other models on SemEval tasks [23,24]
DecAttn	A self-trained supervised algorithm only based on word and phrase alignments which are used to partition the problem into subtasks [11]
MPCNN	As a self-trained supervised algorithm, Multi-Perspective Convolutional Neural Networks are a CNN specifically tuned for semantic similarities [8]
PWIM and Subword PWIM	As a self-trained supervised algorithm, Pairwise Word Interaction Model (PWIM) is similar to MPCNNs, but directly applies word-interaction computations on the individual word context representations of the given sentences [12]. The Subword PWIM model uses the same functionality but has been adapted to work with character sequence embeddings [28]
Random Forest	Self-trained supervised algorithm that creates multiple trees on specific subsets of the sample data and aggregates the results. We apply the NLP features proposed at SemEval 2017 [29]
SSE	As a self-trained supervised algorithm, Shortcut-stacked Sentence Encoder is an ML approach originally developed for multi-domain natural language inference tasks [10]
Tree LSTM	A self-trained supervised algorithm that processes sentences according to the syntactic sentence structure [9]
Word Aligner	This is a non-trained model that has worked very well on previous similarity tasks outside the RE world [30,31]

Our goal is to analyze *semantic similarity algorithms*
for the purpose of *evaluating and comparing their performances*
with respect to *the accuracy of their predicted semantic similarity scores*
from the point of view of *laymen*
in the context of *natural language requirements pairs with human-annotated semantic similarity labels.*

4.2   Research Questions

In this work, we focus on the following research questions:

– **RQ1:** How do semantic similarity algorithms trained on non-requirements data perform in comparison to algorithms trained on requirements data?
– **RQ2:** Which algorithm performs most accurately for predicting the semantic similarities of natural language requirements?

4.3   Metrics

In order to answer the research questions, we test and analyze the performance of each algorithm based on its semantic similarity prediction accuracy. For this, we apply mean squared error (for a discussion of the adequacy, check [34]) as the performance metric for the algorithms, where n indicates the number of samples and y_i and $\hat{y}_i$ represent the expected and the predicted scores respectively:

$$\text{MSE} = \frac{1}{n} \sum_{i=1}^{n} (y_i - \hat{y}_i)^2$$

4.4   Experiment Design and Execution

The overall procedure of our experiment is illustrated in Fig. 1 and will be further explained in the following sections.

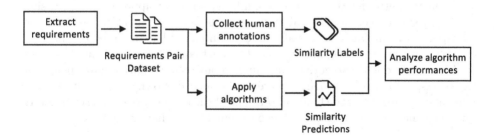

Fig. 1. Overview of the experiment procedure

Requirements Pair Dataset and Human Similarity Annotations. In order to collect human scores, we extract requirements from several requirements specifications and assemble 1000 different requirements pairs. We upload this dataset to the crowdsourcing marketplace *Amazon Mechanical Turk*[1] where human workers, called *turkers,* assign semantic similarity scores to each of our requirements pairs. For each requirements pair, we collect annotations from five different workers and take the median. Annotators are asked to assign a semantic similarity category $S \in \{0, 1, 2, 3, 4, 5\}$ to each requirements pair according to the similarity definition given in Table 1. We argue that this does not require the participants to have any expertise in the domains of linguistics or requirements analysis (c.f. Dagan et al. [35]).

---

[1] https://www.mturk.com/ (accessed 06 February 2019).

We choose to retrieve annotations this way due to the findings of Agirre et al. in the context of their preparations for the SemEval workshops. They have shown that similarity scores with good rates of agreement among the annotators can be observed for similar semantic similarity annotation tasks (cf. e.g. Sect. 2.1).

Each turker who participates in our task on Amazon Mechanical Turk gets paid $0.04 per annotated requirements pair. The total number of annotations per worker over all of our uploaded requirements pairs is not restricted, however, one particular worker can only annotate each requirements pair once.

Similarity Annotation Retrieval. We executed several trial runs with only five requirements pairs each. This is intended to evaluate and compare the performance of the turkers, which enabled us to evaluate the required qualification for the turkers. When we required masters qualification from our turkers, the turkers provided us annotations on average close to our own similarity estimations for the corresponding requirements pairs.

Algorithm Application and Performance Comparison. Afterwards, we apply a variety of different algorithms on this dataset in order to compare their performances.

Balancing. We collect annotations in batches of 100 sentence pairs each, which allows us to control for the balance of similarity scores by appropriately choosing the requirements pairs for our subsequent batches. This means that we check the distribution of similarity scores after every completed batch. Based on that, we create the next batch with more pairs of the less frequent categories and less pairs of the more frequent categories according to our own similarity judgements for the corresponding requirements. However, because our own assessment of these pairs may diverge from the final annotations of the turkers, we cannot completely influence and control the final balance of semantic similarity scores.

Randomization. Before we upload our dataset to Amazon Mechanical Turk, we shuffle the requirements pairs in each batch so that requirements taken from the same document are less likely to be clustered together.

4.5   Study Subjects

Due to Amazon Mechanical Turk, our subjects are primarily laymen. In trial runs, we have retrieved the best results regarding the agreement among annotators when requiring a so-called Masters qualification. Consequently, we take this as a prerequisite for our tasks.

4.6   Study Objects

Our objects are requirements that we extract from 14 different requirements specifications available on the Natural Language Requirements Dataset [36]. These include both real-world industrial requirements specifications and specifications from university projects. We select the software requirements specifications based on our impression of how suitable their requirements would be for getting annotated by laymen. Accordingly, the requirements to be incorporated in our dataset must be understandable without a background briefing. However, we incorporate both requirements that are easy to understand as well as requirements that are more complicated based on their sentence structure and content. Table 3 shows all of the requirements documents that we use for collecting requirements for our dataset.

Table 3. Sources of the requirements in our evaluation dataset

Document	Domain	Number of req.
Pontis	Highway bridge information management system	274
E-store	Online store for consumer electronics	112
Sprat	Goals and scenario management tool	98
NASA	Spacecraft software	86
TCS	Aircraft control software	75
Nenios	Child care management software	71
agentMom	Multi agent communication systems	59
Philips	Messenger software application	42
Mahjong	Web software system for Chinese board game	37
Digital home	Home management system	35
Puget sound	Courseware system	32
Blit	Laboratory information system	29
Colorcast	Web application for paint selection	26
Video search	Video search software	24

As described before, we balance the number of future semantic similarity scores to the extent possible while building the requirements pair dataset based on our own similarity estimations. However, this is difficult because we cannot predict the scores that will be obtained from the annotators. Hence, our evaluation dataset turned out to have a higher number of requirements pairs annotated with the similarity categories 1 or 2, whereas especially the number of requirements pairs annotated with category 4 is small compared to this. The histogram of received semantic similarity categories is illustrated in Fig. 2.

5   Results

In this section, we report the performances of our applied algorithms on our created requirements pair dataset based on the defined metrics and appropriate visualizations.

5.1   Presentation of Results

In the following, we present the performance accuracies of the algorithms introduced in the Sect. 3 when applied to our assembled requirements pair dataset.

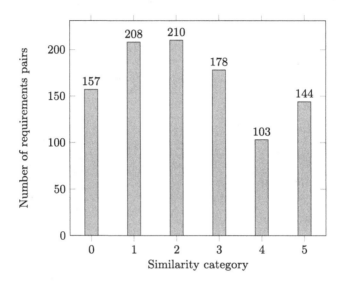

Fig. 2. Distribution of requirements pairs over similarity categories

Performance Accuracy. As described in Sect. 4.3, we use the mean squared error (MSE) as the performance metric to measure the accuracy of the predictions of our applied algorithms based on the collected similarity labels for our requirements evaluation dataset.

Overall and Weighted Mean Squared Error Metrics. Because of the unbalanced distribution of requirements pairs over the six similarity categories, only regarding the overall mean squared error would give a distorted result since there would be a bias towards the more frequent categories. Thus, we calculate the weighted mean squared error by summing up the individual mean squared errors MSE_c for each semantic similarity category c of requirements pairs which have been labeled with this category and dividing this result by 6 according to the number of similarity categories:

$$\text{weighted MSE} = \frac{1}{6} * \sum_{c=0}^{5} \mathrm{MSE}_c$$

We include the overall mean squared error as well as the weighted mean squared error for each algorithm in Table 4 denoted as MSE and MSE_w.

The smaller the mean squared error, the less do the algorithms' predictions diverge from the assigned similarity labels treated as the ground truth. Accordingly, smaller MSEs indicate better algorithm performances.

Performance Results. In Table 4 we list the mean squared error values for every algorithm as described before. We denote the adjusted algorithm settings (where we chose hyper-parameters for the algorithms) by adding *(a)* to the corresponding model names.

5.2   Answers to Research Questions

In this section, we answer our research questions which have been introduced in the previous chapter on the basis of the experiment results presented above.

We will describe the differences between the algorithms relative to each other. Therefore, when we say that the MSE of an algorithm is relatively small or relatively big this refers to the comparison of its performance to the other algorithms.

RQ1: How Do Semantic Similarity Algorithms Trained on Non-requirements Data Perform in Comparison to Algorithms Trained on Requirements Data? For answering this research question, we only consider our self-trained algorithms and the pre-trained sentence encoders because the monolingual word aligner and the baseline algorithms do not need to be trained.

From analyzing the mean squared error results of these algorithms, it can be inferred that most of the evaluated models perform rather well in the context of this work because the majority of the weighted mean squared error values is below or around 1.5. This means that on average the predictions of the corresponding algorithms do not diverge much more than one similarity category from the expected similarity score as interpreted by humans.

In particular, the pre-trained Word-trigram sentence encoder model with both its original and adjusted application settings shows a very good performance on our requirements data, achieving a weighted mean squared error of 0.94 with its adjusted settings and of 0.96 with the standard model. Behind these two model versions, the BiLSTM Avg model ranks third among all trained algorithms and completes the set of the best three algorithms within this experiment, producing prediction results with a weighted MSE of 0.98.

As can be seen in Table 4, for almost all of the trained algorithms we were able to come up with adjusted training or application settings so that better performances on the evaluation dataset could be achieved. For example, especially for the Subword PWIM and the standard PWIM models, the performance differences between the unadjusted and the adjusted settings are very large.

Table 4. Table shows performances on our requirements evaluation dataset ordered by weighted mean squared error. Models that have been self-trained or applied with adjusted settings are marked with (a).

Algorithm	MSE	MSE$_w$	Type
Word-trigram (a)	0.96	0.94	Pre-Trained
Char ngram BOW	0.94	0.94	Baseline
Word-trigram	0.95	0.96	Pre-Trained
BiLSTM Avg	0.98	0.98	Pre-Trained
Charagram (a)	0.97	1.06	Pre-Trained
Charagram	0.95	1.08	Pre-Trained
Word Aligner (a)	0.99	1.10	Non-Trained
InferSent (a)	1.10	1.14	Pre-Trained
Word Aligner	1.03	1.15	Non-Trained
Subword PWIM (a)	1.20	1.15	Self-Trained
PWIM (a)	1.20	1.16	Self-Trained
Random Forest (a)	1.29	1.21	Self-Trained
Word2vec CBOW	1.25	1.28	Baseline
MPCNN (a)	1.33	1.29	Self-Trained
USE (a)	1.28	1.30	Pre-Trained
USE	1.29	1.31	Pre-Trained
Random Forest	1.38	1.31	Self-Trained
SSE (a)	1.49	1.36	Self-Trained
Tree LSTM (a)	1.44	1.45	Self-Trained
PWIM	1.64	1.56	Self-Trained
Subword PWIM	1.78	1.63	Self-Trained
MPCNN	1.75	1.63	Self-Trained
SSE	1.98	1.85	Self-Trained
Tree LSTM	2.17	2.03	Self-Trained
DecAttn (a)	2.59	2.50	Self-Trained
InferSent	2.77	2.55	Pre-Trained
DecAttn	3.08	2.90	Self-Trained

RQ2: Which Algorithm Performs Most Accurately for Predicting the Semantic Similarities of Natural Language Requirements? The best-performing algorithms in our experiment were the adjusted Word-trigram model and the Char ngram BOW baseline which both achieved the smallest weighted MSE of 0.94.

Furthermore, the third best algorithm, the BiLSTM Avg model, completes the set of algorithms which reached a weighted MSEs below 1.0. This approach provides slightly better results for the lower similarity categories 0, 1 and 2 but performs less accurately for the other, higher similarity categories.

Apart from this, when further analyzing Table 4, it can be seen that there are more algorithms whose performances do not greatly differ from the best results described above.

All in all, despite the minor differences to other model performances, our experiment results have shown that the Word-trigram and the Char ngram BOW models perform most accurately within the scope of this experiment.

6   Interpretation

In this section, we interpret the results and observations described before for each individual research question. Furthermore, we discuss the threats to validity which apply to our conducted experiment.

6.1   RQ1: How Do Semantic Similarity Algorithms Trained on Non-requirements Data Perform in Comparison to Algorithms Trained on Requirements Data?

Our experiment reveals that distinct trained semantic similarity algorithms achieve very different performances. Within this section, we identify and discuss various findings regarding the characteristics of these algorithms and their influence on the performance results.

For our self-trained models, we used the same training data, classification layer, loss function, and training objective. However, these models exhibit substantially different performances. Thus, we conclude, that the actual architecture (esp. of neural networks) of the underlying models impacts accuracy.

Algorithms that do not consider the word order can perform equal or better than algorithms sensitive to the word order. This is especially true for the bag of words based algorithms. Thus, we conclude that word order is not important to detect similar requirements, in contrast to other NLP tasks.

We adjusted the parameters of various algorithms to make them perform better on requirements data. This included the pre-processing steps. Thereby we noticed that for the different algorithms, different pre-processing steps have a positive influence on their accuracy. However, the best choices of pre-processing steps which yield the highest performance gains largely differ between models. We assume that this is likely linked to the way of how models process the input texts and how they model input representations so that, for instance, some models prefer to keep stop words and original word forms in order to better understand sentence structures and word relationships.

6.2   RQ2: Which Algorithm Performs Most Accurately for Predicting the Semantic Similarities of Natural Language Requirements?

As already identified in Sect. 5.2, the models with the best overall performance in our experiment are the Word-trigram and Char ngram BOW models. In the following we further discuss these algorithms and their performances.

We believe that the Word-trigram model might perform better than the Char ngram BOW baseline when they are both applied to other datasets by using the same implementation settings like in our experiment. This is because the Word-trigram model has already proven its transferability from its training dataset to another dataset, that is, our requirements dataset whereas the settings of the Char ngram BOW model are completely adjusted and dependent on our evaluation dataset.

For this reason, we consider the Word-trigram model as the best overall model not only because it outperformed all other models applied within our experiment, but also because of its proven transferability. Moreover, we think that its large paraphrase training corpus and the combination of word and character embeddings allow it to capture important and meaningful characteristics of words and sentences that are crucial for the determination of semantic similarity. Because of this embedding information, we assume that this model can better capture important word semantics and semantic relations between words compared to the simpler token occurrence-based approaches which merely rely on lexical token overlaps. This might be even more important for other requirements specifications which may use less consistent terminology.

6.3   Threats to Validity

We discuss the validity threats according to the different issues described by Wohlin [32].

Reliability of Measures. In our experiment, we apply the ordinal similarity scale which is used to collect human interpretations of semantic similarity for given requirements pairs. This measure can be unreliable because humans may interpret semantic similarities differently. However, we collect similarity annotations from five different raters for every requirements pair and take the median in order to retrieve the final similarity label.

The inter-rater agreement according to the Kendall's coefficient of concordance W of 0.607 suggests that there is a correlation between the scores of the different annotators for each requirements pair. Thus, there is a good degree of agreement between the raters regarding the semantic similarities of our requirements pairs which is why we assume that reasonable similarity labels have been obtained.

Finally, we review the obtained dataset. We note that while some scores diverge from how we would have rated the corresponding requirements pairs, the majority of these labels agrees with our own point of view. Consequently, despite the sometimes large divergences between the individual annotations of different raters, we argue that we have retrieved a suitable dataset for the purpose of this study where the potential disagreement between raters is counteracted by taking the median score.

Random Irrelevancies in Experimental Setting. This issue is concerned with possible influences on the result due to external disturbances like noise or interruptions. Since our subjects can log on to Amazon Mechanical Turk and participate in our experiment from any place and at any time, we cannot control their environment and outside influences.

Random Heterogeneity of Subjects. Since all Amazon Mechanical Turk workers who fulfill the defined qualification requirements of our experiment are able to accept and participate in our created task, there might be a certain heterogeneity of subjects.

We tried to mitigate the effects of individual differences by requiring the Master qualification as well as by taking the median from five different annotators for every requirements pair. Furthermore, we conducted several trial runs for obtaining similarity annotations where we investigated and selected the most suitable qualification requirements In these trial runs, the median value of the obtained scores for the best selected qualification requirements seemed to be reasonable and suitable for the tested pairs.

Mono-operation Bias. The mono-operation bias describes the problem of not representing the construct broadly enough, for instance, by only including one subject, variable or object. In our experiment, we only used requirements from the domain of information technology. Hence, results might not generalize.

Mixed Scales. In our experiment, we use an ordinal similarity scale to record the similarity annotations assigned by our subjects so that every annotation corresponds to one of the six similarity categories. Our applied algorithms produce predictions according to a similar idea of similarity, however, their similarity estimations are continuous so that they can lay between categories and thus correspond to an interval scale. Since we calculate the mean squared error based on the ordinal human similarity annotations and the continuous algorithm predictions, we compare values from an ordinal scale to values from an interval scale. This constitutes an error according to measure theory and thus poses a threat to the validity of our results.

Interaction of Selection and Treatment. In our case, we utilized laymen as subjects for our study. However, the study results are intended for evaluating the suitability of the tested semantic similarity algorithms for requirements engineering in industry where requirements analysts and experts are concerned with the topic of semantic similarities of requirements. Due to their background knowledge and experience, requirements experts might interpret semantic similarities of requirements differently than laymen. Thus, this might negatively influence the generalizability of our results to industrial practice.

Interaction of Setting and Treatment. This threat concerns the risk of using a different experimental setting or relying on non-representative objects during the study compared to what is standard in industrial practice. In our experiment, we used requirements from industrial requirements specifications or specifications from university that are similar to industrial specifications. Most of these specifications have been created for real-life projects. Thus, we believe that they are at least to some extent representative of requirements used in industrial practice.

7   Summary

In this work, we researched and investigated suitable approaches for automatically estimating the semantic similarities of requirements pairs. In order to evaluate and compare these approaches, we designed an experiment in which the algorithms' predictions were measured against human similarity interpretations that were treated as the ground truth. For this purpose, we assembled an evaluation requirements dataset containing 1000 distinct requirements pairs which were extracted from several requirements specifications for industrial and university projects. For this dataset, we obtained similarity labels from human annotators according to an ordinal similarity scale from 0 to 5 using Amazon Mechanical Turk as a crowdsourcing platform.

The requirements pair dataset was used to determine the performances of our selected and applied algorithms by calculating the mean squared error between their predictions and the corresponding human similarity labels. Due to the unbalanced distribution of the requirements pairs in our evaluation dataset over the similarity categories, we calculated a weighted mean squared error which determines and averages individual MSE values for each similarity class. Based on these performance results, we were able to draw different conclusions regarding our research questions which we summarize in the following.

RQ1: How do Semantic Similarity Algorithms Trained on Non-requirements Data Perform in Comparison to Algorithms Trained on Requirements Data? We found that the different algorithms perform very differently on requirements data both regarding their overall performances as well as regarding their performances for individual similarity categories. This indicated that the models have different prediction tendencies regarding the various similarity categories. Furthermore, we suggested that the performances of algorithms which do not capture characteristics about word order and sentence structures do not seem to be negatively influenced because these types of information do not seem to noticeably affect the semantic similarity of requirements pairs.

RQ2: Which Algorithm Performs Most Accurately for Predicting the Semantic Similarities of Natural Language Requirements? In our study, the Word-trigram sentence encoder model developed by Wieting et al. [23] as well as the Char ngram BOW baseline approach achieved the best overall performance accuracy with a weighted mean squared error of 0.94. The Word-trigram model combines word embeddings with character trigram embeddings and averages these combinations in order to retrieve sentence vector representations whereas the Char ngram BOW method is based on lexical character sequence overlaps. Despite the equal performance results, we believe that the Word-trigram model would provide better performances in practice due to its use of token embeddings which capture individual word and sentence semantics instead of just relying on token occurrences and overlaps.

References

1. Femmer, H., Vogelsang, A.: Requirements quality is quality in use. IEEE Softw. **36**(3), 83–91 (2018)
2. Femmer, H., Fernández, D.M., Wagner, S., Eder, S.: Rapid quality assurance with requirements smells. J. Syst. Softw. **123**, 190–213 (2017)
3. Femmer, H.: Automatic requirements reviews - potentials, limitations and practical tool support. In: Felderer, M., Méndez Fernández, D., Turhan, B., Kalinowski, M., Sarro, F., Winkler, D. (eds.) PROFES 2017. LNCS, vol. 10611, pp. 617–620. Springer, Cham (2017). https://doi.org/10.1007/978-3-319-69926-4_53
4. Wiegers, K.E., Beatty, J.: Software Requirements. Microsoft Press, Redmond (2013)
5. Natt och Dag, J., Regnell, B., Carlshamre, P., Andersson, M., Karlsson, J.: A feasibility study of automated natural language requirements analysis in market-driven development. Requir. Eng. **7**(1), 20–33 (2002)
6. Silver, D., et al.: Mastering the game of go with deep neural networks and tree search. Nature **529**(7587), 484 (2016)
7. Cer, D., Diab, M., Agirre, E., Lopez-Gazpio, I., Specia, L.: SemEval-2017 task 1: semantic textual similarity multilingual and crosslingual focused evaluation. In: Proceedings of the 11th International Workshop on Semantic Evaluation (SemEval 2017), pp. 1–14. Association for Computational Linguistics (2017)
8. He, H., Gimpel, K., Lin, J.: Multi-perspective sentence similarity modeling with convolutional neural networks. In: Proceedings of the 2015 Conference on Empirical Methods in Natural Language Processing, Association for Computational Linguistics, pp. 1576–1586 (2015)
9. Tai, K.S., Socher, R., Manning, C.D.: Improved semantic representations from tree-structured long short-term memory networks. CoRR abs/1503.00075 (2015)
10. Nie, Y., Bansal, M.: Shortcut-stacked sentence encoders for multi-domain inference. In: Proceedings of the 2nd Workshop on Evaluating Vector Space Representations for NLP, pp. 41–45. Association for Computational Linguistics (2017)
11. Parikh, A., Täckström, O., Das, D., Uszkoreit, J.: A decomposable attention model for natural language inference. In: Proceedings of the 2016 Conference on Empirical Methods in Natural Language Processing, pp. 2249–2255. Association for Computational Linguistics (2016)
12. He, H., Lin, J.: Pairwise word interaction modeling with deep neural networks for semantic similarity measurement. In: Proceedings of the 2016 Conference of the North American Chapter of the Association for Computational Linguistics: Human Language Technologies, pp. 937–948. Association for Computational Linguistics (2016)

13. Mihany, F.A., Moussa, H., Kamel, A., Ezat, E.: A framework for measuring similarity between requirements documents. In: Proceedings of the 10th International Conference on Informatics and Systems. INFOS 2016, pp. 334–335. ACM, New York (2016)
14. Mihany, F.A., Moussa, H., Kamel, A., Ezzat, E., Ilyas, M.: An automated system for measuring similarity between software requirements. In: Proceedings of the 2nd Africa and Middle East Conference on Software Engineering, AMECSE 2016, pp. 46–51. ACM New York (2016)
15. Natt och Dag, J., Gervasi, V., Brinkkemper, S., Regnell, B.: Speeding up requirements management in a product software company: linking customer wishes to product requirements through linguistic engineering. In: Proceedings of 12th IEEE International Requirements Engineering Conference, September 2004, pp. 283–294 (2004)
16. Natt och Dag, J., Regnell, B., Gervasi, V., Brinkkemper, S.: A linguistic-engineering approach to large-scale requirements management. IEEE Softw. **22**(1), 32–39 (2005)
17. Hayes, J.H., Dekhtyar, A., Sundaram, S.K.: Advancing candidate link generation for requirements tracing: the study of methods. IEEE Trans. Softw. Eng. **32**(1), 4–19 (2006)
18. Eder, S., Femmer, H., Hauptmann, B., Junker, M.: Configuring latent semantic indexing for requirements tracing. In: Proceedings of the Second International Workshop on Requirements Engineering and Testing, RET 2015, pp. 27–33. IEEE Press, Piscataway (2015)
19. Mezghani, M., Kang, J., Sèdes, F.: Industrial requirements classification for redundancy and inconsistency detection in SEMIOS. In: 26th IEEE International Requirements Engineering Conference, RE 2018, Banff, AB, Canada, 20–24 August 2018, pp. 297–303 (2018)
20. Juergens, E., et al.: Can clone detection support quality assessments of requirements specifications? In: Proceedings of the 32nd ACM/IEEE International Conference on Software Engineering - Volume 2, ICSE 2010, pp. 79–88. ACM, New York (2010)
21. Falessi, D., Cantone, G., Canfora, G.: Empirical principles and an industrial case study in retrieving equivalent requirements via natural language processing techniques. IEEE Trans. Softw. Eng. **39**(1), 18–44 (2013)
22. Agirre, E., Diab, M., Cer, D., Gonzalez-Agirre, A.: SemEval-2012 task 6: a pilot on semantic textual similarity. In: Proceedings of the First Joint Conference on Lexical and Computational Semantics - Volume 1: Proceedings of the Main Conference and the Shared Task, and Volume 2: Proceedings of the Sixth International Workshop on Semantic Evaluation, SemEval 2012, pp. 385–393. Association for Computational Linguistics, Stroudsburg (2012)
23. Wieting, J., Gimpel, K.: Pushing the limits of paraphrastic sentence embeddings with millions of machine translations. CoRR abs/1711.05732 (2017)
24. Wieting, J., Mallinson, J., Gimpel, K.: Learning paraphrastic sentence embeddings from back-translated bitext. In: Proceedings of Empirical Methods in Natural Language Processing. (2017)
25. Wieting, J., Bansal, M., Gimpel, K., Livescu, K.: Charagram: embedding words and sentences via character n-grams. CoRR abs/1607.02789 (2016)

26. Conneau, A., Kiela, D., Schwenk, H., Barrault, L., Bordes, A.: Supervised learning of universal sentence representations from natural language inference data. In: Proceedings of the 2017 Conference on Empirical Methods in Natural Language Processing, Copenhagen, Denmark, September 2017, pp. 670–680. Association for Computational Linguistics (2017)

27. Cer, D., et al.: Universal sentence encoder. CoRR abs/1803.11175 (2018)

28. Lan, W., Xu, W.: Character-based neural networks for sentence pair modeling. In: Proceedings of the 2018 Conference of the North American Chapter of the Association for Computational Linguistics: Human Language Technologies, Volume 2 (Short Papers), pp. 157–163. Association for Computational Linguistics (2018)

29. Al-Natsheh, H.T., Martinet, L., Muhlenbach, F., ZIGHED, D.A.: UdL at SemEval-2017 task 1: semantic textual similarity estimation of English sentence pairs using regression model over pairwise features. In: Proceedings of the 11th International Workshop on Semantic Evaluation (SemEval-2017), Vancouver, Canada, August 2017, pp. 115–119. Association for Computational Linguistics (2017)

30. Brychcín, T., Svoboda, L.: UWB at SemEval-2016 task 1: semantic textual similarity using lexical, syntactic, and semantic information. In: SemEval@NAACL-HLT, pp. 588–594. The Association for Computer Linguistics (2016)

31. Sultan, M.A., Bethard, S., Sumner, T.: Back to basics for monolingual alignment: exploiting word similarity and contextual evidence. Trans. Assoc. Comput. Linguist. **2**, 219–230 (2014)

32. Wohlin, C., Runeson, P., Höst, M., Ohlsson, M.C., Regnell, B., Wesslén, A.: Experimentation in Software Engineering. Springer, Heidelberg (2012). https://doi.org/10.1007/978-3-642-29044-2

33. Basili, V.R., Caldiera, G.: Rombach, D.H.: The goal question metric approach. In: Encyclopedia of Software Engineering, pp. 528–532 (1994)

34. Shepperd, M., MacDonell, S.: Evaluating prediction systems in software project estimation. Inf. Softw. Technol. **54**(8), 820–827 (2012)

35. Dagan, I., Dolan, B., Magnini, B., Roth, D.: Recognizing textual entailment: rational, evaluation and approaches. J. Nat. Lang. Eng. **4**, I-Xvii (2010)

36. Ferrari, A., Spagnolo, G.O., Gnesi, S.: PURE: a dataset of public requirements documents. In: IEEE 25th International Requirements Engineering Conference (RE), pp. 502–505. IEEE (2017)

Software Quality Assurance Concepts

On Identifying Similarities in Git Commit Trends—A Comparison Between Clustering and SimSAX

Miroslaw Ochodek[1]([✉]), Miroslaw Staron[2], and Wilhelm Meding[3]

[1] Poznan University of Technology, Poznań, Poland
miroslaw.ochodek@cs.put.poznan.pl
[2] Chalmers | University of Gothenburg, Gothenburg, Sweden
miroslaw.staron@gu.se
[3] Ericsson AB, Gothenburg, Sweden
wilhelm.meding@ericsson.com

Abstract. Software products evolve increasingly fast as markets continuously demand new features and agility to customer's need. This evolution of products triggers an evolution of software development practices in a different way. Compared to classical methods, where products were developed in projects, contemporary methods for continuous integration, delivery, and deployment develop products as part of continuous programs. In this context, software architects, designers, and quality engineers need to understand how the processes evolve over time since there is no natural start and stop of projects. For example, they need to know how similar two iterations of the same program or how similar two development programs are. In this paper, we compare three methods for calculating the degree of similarity between projects by comparing their Git commit series. We test three approaches—the DNA-motifs-inspired SimSAX measure and clustering of subsequences (k-Means and Hierarchical clustering). Our results show that the clustering algorithms are much more sensitive to parameters and often find similarities that are not correct. SimSAX, on the other hand, can be calibrated to find fewer similarities between the projects; the similarities are also more consistent for SimSAX than they are for the clustering. We conclude that it is better to use DNA-inspired motifs as they provide more accurate results.

1 Introduction

Understanding similarity between software development projects is important while performing many important tasks that require projecting historical data to a currently developed project, e.g., predicting defect inflow based on history, predicting development effort, benchmarking productivity of project teams, or evaluating whether the practices of one project apply to another one.

The state-of-the-art approaches to assess similarities between projects focus on *cross-sectional* evaluation. For instance, in the studies on effort estimation each project is usually described by a set of attributes (e.g., size of the product,

© Springer Nature Switzerland AG 2020
D. Winkler et al. (Eds.): SWQD 2020, LNBIP 371, pp. 109–120, 2020.
https://doi.org/10.1007/978-3-030-35510-4_7

business domain, technology) and unsupervised methods such as clustering are often used to construct homogeneous training data sets (e.g., [3,17]).

However, modern software development requires continuous evolution of software products. Mobile Apps, Cloud systems and even embedded software systems evolve continuously [4,5]. The products are often developed using processes that are iterative, responsive to customer needs and often continuous—for example, Agile and Lean software development. In the context of these processes, the notion of software project has been replaced by the notion of software programs. In software development programs, the companies do not plan the number of iterations á priori, but new features are developed as soon as one of the teams is ready to develop them.

Consequently, there is a need to continuously monitor when the products and processes evolved so much that new methods for product quality need to be introduced, the old ones need to be evolved or abandoned. The quality managers need to understand when to change their baselines for comparing between projects so that their assessment is more accurate (e.g., for defect predictions [15]). Therefore, there is a need to find similarities in the way given characteristics of projects change over time rather than focusing on cross-sectional similarities.

In this paper, we set-off to compare three methods of finding similarities in Git commit histories (the number of commits in time), which are two state-of-the-art clustering methods—k-Means and hierarchical clustering [2,10] and using two popular distance measures—Euclidean distance and Dynamic Time Wrapping (DTW) with the recently proposed SimSAX measure [14]. We use Git commit histories from two Eclipse sub-projects (JDT and Platform) as objects of the study. Since ground truth allowing to evaluate the accuracy of the compared methods is not available, we focus on understanding the pros and cons of applying each of the methods. We use simulations to generate a set of parameters for the methods and show which similarities these methods discover. As the criteria for comparison between these methods, we use the *percentage of similar weeks*. The similarity of project A to project B is then defined as the percentage of the weeks in project A that are similar to weeks in project B.

Our results show that the clustering algorithms are much more sensitive to parameters and often find similarities that are not correct. SimSAX, on the other hand, can be calibrated to find fewer similarities between the projects; the similarities are also more consistent for SimSAX than they are for the clustering.

2   Background

2.1   Similarity Between Git Commit Trends

For our work, we use the definition of a time series $T = t_1, ..., t_m$ as an ordered set of m real-valued variables. A Git commits history can be regarded as a time series if we consider *the number of commits in time*. We will refer to such time series being the number of commits per week as a *Git commits trend*. We do not take into account any other meta data available in Git commit histories.

We are interested in finding *similar* subsequences of a length w of two Git commits trends T_i and T_j ($w < m_i$ and $w < m_j$, where m_i, m_j are the lengths of T_i and T_j). The similarity of project A to project B is then defined as the percentage of the weeks in project A that are similar to weeks in project B, compared to the total number of weeks in project A. We consider similarity as the similarity of shapes, which means that two time-series are matched as well as possible, by a non-linear stretching and contracting of the time axes [2].

2.2   Time-Series Clustering

Time-series clustering is, in general, an unsupervised machine-learning method that partition a given set of time series in such a way that homogenous time series are grouped together based on a certain similarity measure [2]. We can cluster subsequences of many time series to find clusters that group subsequences between these time series. Two most popular families of clustering algorithms are hierarchical and partitioning clustering.

Hierarchical clustering makes a hierarchy of clusters using agglomerative or divisive algorithms. Agglomerative algorithms consider each time series as a cluster, and then gradually merges the clusters. Divisive algorithms start by grouping all of the time series in a single cluster and then split the cluster to reach the clusters containing a single time series. We selected the agglomerative hierarchical clustering method using Ward variance minimization algorithm as a representative algorithm for this family of algorithms.

Partitioning clustering algorithms make k groups from n unlabelled time series in the way that each group contains at least one time series. One of the most frequently used algorithms of this type is k-Means. We use this algorithm as a representative of the family of partitioning clustering methods.

All of the mentioned clustering algorithms require similarity measures to compare time series. We use two most popular shape-based similarity measures— Euclidean distance and LB_Keogh, which is a lower bounding measure for Dynamic Time Warping (DTW) [8].

2.3   Similarity-based on Symbolic Aggregate approXimation

$SimSAX_{n,w,a}$ (Similarity-based on Symbolic Aggregate approXimation) is a measure of time-series similarity, originally proposed to find similarities between defect-inflow profiles [14]. The measure is inspired by the research on DNA sequence alignment in the area of bioinformatics.

The process of calculating $SimSAX_{n,w,a}$ is multi-staged and involves a transformation of the original Git commits trend into a sequence of symbols. In the first step, we transform a sequence of numbers into a sequence of symbols using Symbolic Aggregate approXimation (SAX) [11]. The method operates on moving windows of a given length n (each window is normalized to have a mean of zero and standard deviation of one) and transforms each of them into a word of length w using symbols from an alphabet of size a. Then, Piecewise Aggregate Approximation (PAA) [9] is applied to reduce its dimensionality from n to w.

During this stage, the window is divided into w segments of equal length and each segment is replaced by its mean value. The newly created sequence is further transformed into a word over the alphabet of size a assuming that all the symbols of the alphabet are equiprobable.

When comparing two time series, we compare every pair of the generated windows transformed into words. When all of the symbols match, the verdict is that two windows are similar. They are called *motif*—a recurring subsequence in a time series.

Finally, we calculate $SimSAX_{n,w,a}(A, B)$ for time series A and B as the percentage of weeks covered by the windows coming from the time series A that were indicated as similar to at least one window from time series B (being a motif), and do the same for B. Therefore, the result of calculating $SimSAX_{n,w,a}(A, B)$ is a tuple (X, Y), where X and Y are the percentages of weeks covered by at least one motif in A and B, respectively. For instance, having $SimSAX_{n,w,a}(A, B) = (100\%, 30\%)$ would mean that there is not any novelty in time series A with respect to B, while time series B has 70% of weeks covered by subsequences not observed in A.

An open-source tool allowing to calculate $SimSAX_{n,w,a}(A, B)$ is available on GitHub.[1] The tool allows to calibrate the parameters w and a using simulations.[2]

3   Related Work

There are, basically, three different models for comparing software projects, organizations, and processes.

The first one is to use databases of projects, where users input data about characteristics of their projects, the database selects the most similar projects, which can be used for benchmarking [12]. The advantages are, among others: (i) large number of comparison parameters, and (ii) flexibility in choosing parameters to compare. However, the disadvantage is the need for manual input of parameters and the lack of full data for predictions (e.g., lack of full defect database for predicting defects, or detailed information about requirements).

Another approach is to use similarity measures like Euclidean distance [16] or its derivatives. Such a comparison has the advantage that it is very simple and it can work on time series (e.g., defect inflow, Git commit trend), but it has a disadvantage of being prone to bias caused by discrepancies between individual data points. Often, these techniques are supported by unsupervised machine learning methods such as k-Means or hierarchical clustering to help in grouping similar objects. Similarity measures and clustering algorithms were employed in many studies in the area of effort estimation. For instance, Silhavy et al. [17] and Bardsiri et al. [3] used clustering to find homogeneous sets of projects for training effort estimation models. However, none of these studies considered the change of projects characteristics in time.

---

[1] The SimSAX tool—https://github.com/mochodek/simsax.

[2] More information about calibrating $SimSAX_{n,w,a}(A, B)$ can be found in [14].

The recently proposed $SimSAX_{n,w,a}$ measure [14] was originally designed to find similarities between the ways of working in software development teams based on defect-inflow profiles. In this study, it is applied to find similarities in Git commit trends.

Finally, the third type of approaches to find similarities between software projects are formalizations of processes and their comparison. An example of such a model is the work of van der Alst [1], where two processes are described, formalized and compared. The advantage of this type of models is the accuracy of comparison, but the disadvantage is the need for extensive data collection.

There have been studies that analyzed Git commit histories. For instance, Hindle et al. [6] studied commits with respect to their size and purpose. We can learn from their study that large commits can carry important information about the project and its structure. Similarly, Nayebi et al. [13] studied commits removing the code, tests, libraries, and other artifacts from a product codebase. Although these works show that it is worth to consider the nature of commits while analyzing Git commit histories, in this study, we focus on comparing Git commit trends only from the frequency point of view to limit the axes of analysis since our goal is to comparing different approaches to find similarities rather than study commit histories themselves.

4   Research Design

We perform the simulations on Git commit trend data collected from open source projects. We choose the projects that have been used in previous studies, and that has been found to have good quality, professional development process behind them and which are mature in terms of the number of releases.

We choose a set of Eclipse sub-projects as the objects of the study (we collect their Git commit histories and transform them into time series of numbers of commits per week): Eclipse JDT Core – 872 weeks (from 2001-06-11 to 2018-02-25); Eclipse JDT UI – 877 weeks (from 2001-05-07 to 2018-02-25); Eclipse Platform – 876 weeks (from 2001-05-07 to 2018-02-18); and Eclipse Platform SWT – 876 weeks (from 2001-05-14 to 2018-02-25).

We selected three pairs of projects for the comparison: O_1 – Eclipse JDT Core and Eclipse JDT UI; O_2 – Eclipse JDT Core and Eclipse Platform; and O_3 – Eclipse Platform SWT and Eclipse JDT UI. Pair O_1 consists of commit trends from the same Eclipse sub-project (but different components), while the remaining two (O_2 and O_3) group commit trends from two different sub-projects. Since the development processes are very similar for these products, we should expect to observe high similarity when we try to quantify their similarity.

We generate subsequences of the Git commit time series using 52-week sliding windows; a 52-week window captures the regularity of main releases in the Eclipse project. We capture the releases as we would like to avoid randomness in finding similarities and we focus on complete releases. We standardize each window (normalize to have a mean of zero and standard deviation of one), because we are interested in finding similar shapes regardless of the absolute number of commits.

Having prepared the commit time series, we run the considering methods on each object using the following configurations: Hierarchical clustering, Euclidean—HE1 (k = 34, 43, 41), HE2 (k = 68, 86, 82), HE3 (k = 400), and HE4 (inconsistency); k-Means, DTW—KDTW1 (k = 34, 43, 41), KDTW2 (k = 68, 86, 82), and KDTW3 (k = 400); and $\text{SimSAX}_{n,w=7,a=9}(\text{A}, \text{B})$ (we used SimSAX calibration algorithm to find the parameters w and a [14]).

The well-known drawback of the partitioning clustering methods is that the number of clusters, k, has to be a priori assigned [2]. Although theoretically, the hierarchical clustering methods do not require pre-assigning k, in practice, if one wants to obtain flat clusters some criterion of splitting the hierarchical structure needs to be provided (e.g., by providing a maximum distance between clusters, number of clusters, etc.). In our study, we also use one of the automatic approaches to determine the number of clusters based on inconsistency [7] (however, such methods are known to be imperfect) and variants of the method with the pre-assigned k. For manually assigned k, we test 7 different values, including $k = 400$, which is approximately half of the time series lengths, and theoretically, allows to form clusters containing pairs of similar subsequences.

We use the measure of *week coverage* (WeekCov) to describe the similarity between Git commit trends, which is the percentage of weeks in that time series that are covered by at least one 52-week window indicated as similar between the projects. This is the equivalent of the outcome of $\text{SimSAX}_{n,w,a}(\text{A}, \text{B})$.

In order to compare the methods between projects, we introduce another measure called *windows coverage*—$\text{WindCov}(m_1, m_2)$. We define it as the percentage of 52-week windows indicated as similar by a given method m_1 for the compared pair of projects that are also indicated as similar by the second method m_2. Finally, we use an visual examination to evaluate the outputs of the methods.

5   Results and Discussion

We organize our analysis into week coverage and windows coverage analyses to show how the methods differ in matching the studied pairs of the Git commit time series.

5.1   Week Coverage

The main results of the similarity calculations are in Table 1. Columns refer to different objects (i.e. pairs of projects to compare) and each row is a different algorithm with a different set of parameters.

All of the considered variants of clustering algorithms indicate the percentage week coverage equal, or very close to, 100% (see Table 1). This means that, for all projects considered in our study, these algorithms could find similar windows in another project from the pair that altogether cover all the weeks in that projects. Although the Git commit trends for these projects are very similar, they are not identical. Therefore, such similarity is, naturally, not accurate, as it could mislead further analyses assuming that two projects are identical.

Table 1. Percentage of weeks covered by indicated motifs.

Method	Week coverage O_1			Week coverage O_2			Week coverage O_3		
	Average	A	B	Average	A	B	Average	A	B
Hierarchical, Euc., k = (34, 43, 41)	100%	100%	100%	100%	100%	100%	100%	100%	100%
Hierarchical, Euc., k = (68, 86, 82)	100%	100%	100%	100%	100%	100%	100%	100%	100%
Hierarchical, Euc., k = 400	100%	100%	100%	100%	100%	100%	100%	100%	100%
Hierarchical, Euc., inconsistency	100%	100%	100%	100%	100%	100%	100%	100%	100%
K-means, Euc., k = (34, 43, 41)	100%	100%	100%	100%	100%	100%	100%	100%	100%
K-means, Euc., k = (68, 86, 82)	100%	100%	100%	100%	100%	100%	100%	100%	100%
K-means, Euc., k = 400	100%	100%	100%	100%	99%	100%	100%	100%	100%
K-means, DTW, k = (34, 43, 41)	100%	100%	100%	100%	100%	100%	100%	100%	100%
K-means, DTW, k = (68, 86, 82)	100%	100%	100%	100%	100%	100%	100%	100%	100%
K-means, DTW, k = 400	100%	100%	100%	100%	100%	100%	100%	100%	100%
$SimSAX_{n,7,9}(A, B)$	70%	67%	73%	82.5%	81%	84%	78.5%	80%	77%

The $SimSAX_{n,w,a}$ measure yield different results, which seem more realistic. The week coverage ranged between 67–84%. Also, the indicated similarity is not symmetrical. For instance, for the object O_1, only 67% of weeks of Eclipse JDT Core are covered by similar windows comparing to 73% for Eclipse JDT UI. We make a similar observation for the object O_2 (81% and 84%) and O_3 (80% and 77%). A visual comparison of Eclipse JDT UI (O_1) weeks covered is presented in Fig. 1, where each red line represents one motif/cluster.

We can observe that $SimSAX_{n,w,a}$ is more selective in finding similarities—fewer horizontal red lines in Fig. 1(a). The patterns revolve around peak-like shapes (or even double peaks appearing in close proximity). It also visible that for Eclipse JDT UI these patterns are spread evenly through the whole time series (they cover 73% of the weeks).

In contrast to $SimSAX_{n,w,a}$, the k-Means clustering with Euclidean distance measure (see (c) and (e) in Fig. 1), the pattern gets random and the credibility in the results is lower. The k-Means with Euclidean distance results in too many false positives, which we can see that all weeks are matched to some other weeks—which is not correct as the projects are not identical.

The k-Means clustering with DTW (see (d) and (f) in Fig. 1), results in finding fewer clusters containing windows from both series (fewer horizontal red lines), but still matches all weeks, which results in higher similarity measure than the $SimSAX_{n,w,a}$ measure.

5.2 Comparing Windows Coverage

The comparison of windows coverage (WinCov) is presented in Table 2. Each cell in the table shows how many of the same windows are found by two methods (row and column) with respect to all windows found by the method in the row.

Analyzing the table leads to the observation that with increasing k, the percentage of overlap decreases, showing that the low k is not useful in practice. When a smaller number of clusters was selected (k between 34 and 86), all windows were grouped in clusters containing windows from both projects. When

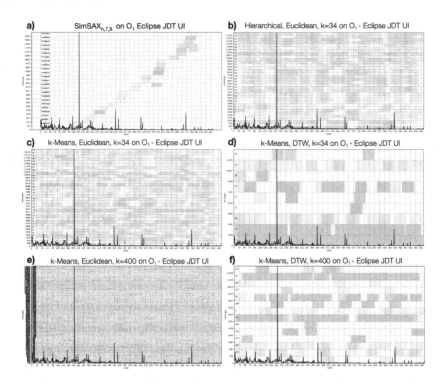

Fig. 1. Examples of weeks covered by similar windows for O_1 (Eclipse JDT UI) indicated by different algorithms (red boxes represent similar windows—y-axis indicates the same cluster/motif). (Color figure online)

k was increased to 400, windows indicated as similar started to differ between Hierarchical clustering and k-Means (e.g., compare HE3 and KE3 in Table 2). SimSAX$_{n,w,a}$ selected visibly fewer windows as similar (5% to 10% of windows indicated by the clustering algorithms).

The differences in how the considered algorithms group windows are shown by examples presented in Fig. 2. The patterns of similar series are overlapping lines with limited dispersion, while the non-similar, false-positive patterns are when lines that are visible different or do not overlap.

The figure shows clusters/motifs from Eclipse JDT Core and JDT UI (O_1) including a selected window of Eclipse JDT Core. It is visible that when k increases, the number of subsequences in clusters decreases.

It also shows that having multiple series in one cluster (small k), results in high coverage of one cluster; since the similarity within the cluster is low, then the similarity for the entire series is not accurate—too many false positive matchings. When increasing the k, we get fewer sub-sequences in the cluster, and therefore, fewer matches in the entire series—thus, fewer false positive matchings. This presence of multiple false positive matchings renders the clustering methods as inadequate for measuring the similarity between Git commit trends.

Table 2. The comparison of the percentage of common windows identified as similar by a method in the row that were also identified as similar by the method in a column.

Object	Symbol	Method	HE1	HE2	HE3	HE4	KE1	KE2	KE3	KDTW1	KDTW2	KDTW3	Sim SAX
O_1	HE1	Hierarchical, Euclidean, k = (34, 43, 41)		100%	88%	97%	100%	100%	83%	100%	100%	99%	5%
O_1	HE2	Hierarchical, Euclidean, k = (68, 86, 82)	100%		88%	97%	100%	100%	83%	100%	100%	99%	5%
O_1	HE3	Hierarchical, Euclidean, k = 400	100%	100%		100%	100%	100%	86%	100%	100%	99%	5%
O_1	HE4	Hierarchical, Euclidean, inconsistency	100%	100%	91%		100%	100%	84%	100%	100%	99%	5%
O_1	KE1	K-means, Euclidean, k = (34, 43, 41)	100%	100%	88%	97%		100%	83%	100%	100%	99%	5%
O_1	KE2	K-means, Euclidean, k = (68, 86, 82)	100%	100%	88%	97%	100%		83%	100%	100%	99%	5%
O_1	KE3	K-means, Euclidean, k = 400	100%	100%	90%	98%	100%	100%		100%	100%	99%	6%
O_1	KDTW1	K-means, DTW, k = (34, 43, 41)	100%	100%	88%	97%	100%	100%	83%		100%	99%	5%
O_1	KDTW2	K-means, DTW, k = (68, 86, 82)	100%	100%	88%	97%	100%	100%	83%	100%		99%	5%
O_1	KDTW3	K-means, DTW, k = 400	100%	100%	88%	97%	100%	100%	83%	100%	100%		5%
O_1	SimSAX	SimSAX$_{n,7,9}$(A, B)	100%	100%	97%	100%	100%	100%	95%	100%	100%	99%	
O_2	HE1	Hierarchical, Euclidean, k = (34, 43, 41)		99%	89%	99%	100%	100%	84%	98%	99%	99%	7%
O_2	HE2	Hierarchical, Euclidean, k = (68, 86, 82)	100%		89%	100%	100%	100%	84%	98%	99%	100%	7%
O_2	HE3	Hierarchical, Euclidean, k = 400	100%	100%		100%	100%	100%	87%	98%	99%	100%	8%
O_2	HE4	Hierarchical, Euclidean, inconsistency	100%	100%	89%		100%	100%	84%	98%	99%	100%	7%
O_2	KE1	K-means, Euclidean, k = (34, 43, 41)	100%	99%	89%	99%		100%	84%	98%	99%	99%	7%
O_2	KE2	K-means, Euclidean, k = (68, 86, 82)	100%	99%	89%	99%	100%		84%	98%	99%	99%	7%
O_2	KE3	K-means, Euclidean, k = 400	100%	100%	92%	100%	100%	100%		98%	99%	100%	8%
O_2	KDTW1	K-means, DTW, k = (34, 43, 41)	100%	99%	88%	99%	100%	100%	84%		99%	99%	7%
O_2	KDTW2	K-means, DTW, k = (68, 86, 82)	100%	99%	89%	99%	100%	100%	84%	98%		99%	7%
O_2	KDTW3	K-means, DTW, k = 400	100%	100%	89%	99%	100%	100%	84%	98%	99%		7%
O_2	SimSAX	SimSAX$_{n,7,9}$(A, B)	100%	100%	97%	100%	100%	100%	90%	96%	100%	100%	
O_3	HE1	Hierarchical, Euclidean, k = (34, 43, 41)		99%	78%	92%	100%	99%	79%	100%	98%	99%	8%
O_3	HE2	Hierarchical, Euclidean, k = (68, 86, 82)	100%		79%	93%	100%	99%	80%	100%	98%	99%	8%
O_3	HE3	Hierarchical, Euclidean, k = 400	100%	100%		99%	100%	99%	85%	100%	98%	99%	10%
O_3	HE4	Hierarchical, Euclidean, inconsistency	100%	100%	84%		100%	99%	81%	100%	98%	99%	9%
O_3	KE1	K-means, Euclidean, k = (34, 43, 41)	100%	99%	78%	92%		99%	79%	100%	98%	99%	8%
O_3	KE2	K-means, Euclidean, k = (68, 86, 82)	100%	99%	79%	93%	100%		79%	100%	98%	99%	8%
O_3	KE3	K-means, Euclidean, k = 400	100%	100%	84%	94%	100%	99%		100%	98%	99%	10%
O_3	KDTW1	K-means, DTW, k = (34, 43, 41)	100%	99%	78%	92%	100%	99%	79%		98%	99%	8%
O_3	KDTW2	K-means, DTW, k = (68, 86, 82)	100%	99%	78%	92%	100%	99%	79%	100%		99%	8%
O_3	KDTW3	K-means, DTW, k = 400	100%	99%	78%	92%	100%	99%	79%	100%	98%		8%
O_3	SimSAX	SimSAX$_{n,7,9}$(A, B)	100%	100%	94%	98%	100%	100%	91%	99%	96%	99%	

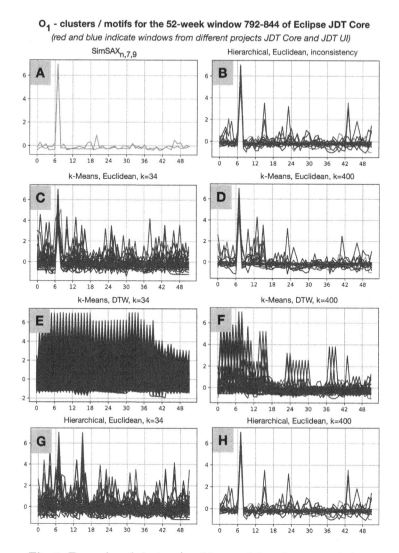

Fig. 2. Examples of clusters/motifs containing the same window.

Finally, we can see in the sub-figure (a) that the calibrated $SimSAX_{n,7,9}$ indicated a motif containing only two windows from both Git commit trends.

5.3 Validity Analysis

We use the framework presented by Wohlin et al. [18] to discuss the threats to validity and our measures to minimize them.

Our main *external validity* threat is the fact that we use a small sample of projects—three pairs—when comparing the algorithms. Essentially, since we are interested in the differences between the methods, we do not need a large sample, but a sample of projects with known similarity. We also need a sample of well-engineered projects and therefore we made a deliberate selection of the sample.

The main *construct validity* threat is the choice of parameters in the study—there is a risk that our choice of parameters is biased towards our method. In order to minimize the probability of this kind of bias, we chose a broad set of sampling base for the parameters—from small values to large values and doubling the values of the parameters. This minimizes this risk.

One of the main *conclusion validity* threat is the lack of statistical analyses of projects. Since our goal is to use well-engineered projects, our sample was small and therefore we prefer to report the values for each pair instead. This minimizes the risk that using statistics for small samples leads to incorrect conclusions.

6   Conclusions

Software products evolve increasingly fast as markets continuously demand new features and agility to customer's need. This evolution of products triggers an evolution of software development practices in a different way. Quantifying similarity between evolved projects is important when comparing projects or using prediction models.

In this paper, we studied three approaches (including a recently proposed one) for quantifying similarity between Git commit trends—k-Means clustering, hierarchical clustering, and $\text{SimSAX}_{n,w,a}$.

Our results show that the $\text{SimSAX}_{n,w,a}$ measure is more selective in finding similarities than the clustering methods. For the projects which are similar, but not identical, it estimates the similarity to be between 67% and 84%, compared to other methods which predicted 100% similarity between these projects.

Clustering methods must group all observations, i.e. both similar and non-similar series. Which means that if we have not enough clusters then we end up with clusters having non-similar series. This means that high week coverage does not mean that the projects are similar. This, in consequence, means that the results of the method are very sensitive to changes in the configuration parameters and therefore less useful in practice.

Euclidean distance and DTW have different properties, but they impact the results in similar ways. DTW is more fragile to trivial matches of moving windows, but groups more subsequences than the Euclidean distance. Thus we see DTW as the better choice for the distance measure (one can consider using moving windows with a stride greater than one).

References

1. van der Aalst, W.M.P., de Medeiros, A.K.A., Weijters, A.J.M.M.: Process equivalence: comparing two process models based on observed behavior. In: Dustdar, S., Fiadeiro, J.L., Sheth, A.P. (eds.) BPM 2006. LNCS, vol. 4102, pp. 129–144. Springer, Heidelberg (2006). https://doi.org/10.1007/11841760_10

2. Aghabozorgi, S., Shirkhorshidi, A.S., Wah, T.Y.: Time-series clustering-a decade review. Inf. Syst. **53**, 16–38 (2015)
3. Bardsiri, V.K., Jawawi, D.N.A., Hashim, S.Z.M., Khatibi, E.: Increasing the accuracy of software development effort estimation using projects clustering. IET Softw. **6**(6), 461–473 (2012)
4. Bosch, J.: Continuous Software Engineering. Springer, Cham (2016). https://doi.org/10.1007/978-3-319-11283-1
5. Bosch, J.: Speed, data, and ecosystems: the future of software engineering. IEEE Softw. **33**(1), 82–88 (2016)
6. Hindle, A., German, D.M., Holt, R.: What do large commits tell us?: a taxonomical study of large commits. In: Proceedings of the 2008 International Working Conference on Mining Software Repositories, pp. 99–108. ACM (2008)
7. Jones, E., Oliphant, T., Peterson, P., et al.: SciPy: Open source scientific tools for Python (2001). http://www.scipy.org/. Accessed 12 Mar 2018
8. Keogh, E., Ratanamahatana, C.A.: Exact indexing of dynamic time warping. Knowl. Inf. Syst. **7**(3), 358–386 (2004)
9. Keogh, E.J., Pazzani, M.J.: A simple dimensionality reduction technique for fast similarity search in large time series databases. In: Terano, T., Liu, H., Chen, A.L.P. (eds.) PAKDD 2000. LNCS (LNAI), vol. 1805, pp. 122–133. Springer, Heidelberg (2000). https://doi.org/10.1007/3-540-45571-X_14
10. Liao, T.W.: Clustering of time series data a survey. Pattern Recogn. **38**(11), 1857–1874 (2005)
11. Lin, J., Keogh, E., Lonardi, S., Chiu, B.: A symbolic representation of time series, with implications for streaming algorithms. In: Proceedings of the 8th ACM SIGMOD Workshop on Research Issues in Data Mining and Knowledge Discovery pp. 2–11. ACM (2003)
12. Lokan, C., Wright, T., Hill, P., Stringer, M.: Organizational benchmarking using the ISBSG data repository. IEEE Softw. **18**(5), 26–32 (2001)
13. Nayebi, M., Kuznetsov, K., Chen, P., Zeller, A., Ruhe, G.: Anatomy of functionality deletion. In: Proceedings of the Conference on Mining Software Repositories (MSR18), Gothenburg, Sweden (2018)
14. Ochodek, M., Staron, M., Meding, W.: SimSAX: a measure of project similarity based on symbolic approximation method and software defect inflow. Inf. Softw. Technol. (2019). http://www.sciencedirect.com/science/article/pii/S0950584919301363
15. Rana, R., Staron, M., Berger, C., Hansson, J., Nilsson, M., Törner, F., Meding, W., Höglund, C.: Selecting software reliability growth models and improving their predictive accuracy using historical projects data. J. Syst. Softw. **98**, 59–78 (2014)
16. Shepperd, M., Schofield, C.: Estimating software project effort using analogies. IEEE Trans. Softw. Eng. **23**(11), 736–743 (1997)
17. Silhavy, R., Silhavy, P., Prokopová, Z.: Evaluating subset selection methods for use case points estimation. Inf. Softw. Technol. **97**, 1–9 (2018)
18. Wohlin, C., Runeson, P., Host, M., Ohlsson, M.C., Regnell, B., Wessln, A.: Experimentation in Software Engineering: An Introduction. Kluwer Academic Publisher, Boston (2000)

Code Reviews, Software Inspections, and Code Walkthroughs: Systematic Mapping Study of Research Topics

Ilenia Fronza[1], Arto Hellas[2], Petri Ihantola[2], and Tommi Mikkonen[2(✉)]

[1] Free University of Bozen-Bolzano, Bozen-Bolzano, Italy
ilenia.fronza@unibz.it
[2] University of Helsinki, Helsinki, Finland
{arto.hellas,petri.ihantola,tommi.mikkonen}@helsinki.fi

Abstract. Code reviews have been used to improve code quality since the 1970s. Most practitioners in the field of software have some experience with respect to the technique. In this mapping study we illustrate what kinds of research questions are addressed in code review literature. The following themes emerged from analysis of 75 original articles: (1) description or comparison of different code review practices, (2) behavior of reviewers (e.g., eye tracking studies), (3) communication and teamwork, (4) outcomes of code reviews (e.g., what kinds of problems are identified), (5) how properties of code to be reviewed affect reviewing, and (6) reasons for conducting code reviews. About half of the studies have been conducted with students and novices. The numbers of industry papers has significantly increased when compared to the previous reviews in the field.

Keywords: Code reviews · Software inspections · Code walkthroughs · Mapping study

1 Introduction

Software engineering has evolved significantly during the last decades. Code review (sometimes called as peer review) is one of the few activities surviving this evolution. Different forms of peer reviewing have been around since the 1970s [1], and practically every software engineer is familiar with the techniques, at least to some extent. Based on the previous literature, the driving force to do code reviews include finding defects, improving code quality, finding alternative solutions, transferring knowledge and improving teams awareness [2].

Code review, or manual inspection of software quality in general are widely studied topics, but systematic literature studies in the field are still rare. Brykczynski [3] conducted a literature review on checklist based quality assurance of software artifacts (i.e., requirements, design, code, testing, documentation, and process). Authors point out, that although some checks should be

© Springer Nature Switzerland AG 2020
D. Winkler et al. (Eds.): SWQD 2020, LNBIP 371, pp. 121–133, 2020.
https://doi.org/10.1007/978-3-030-35510-4_8

automated, all the listed phases of software development are likely to benefit from manual (possibly computer assisted) inspection. More recently, Ebad [4] did a systematic literature review to compare multiple manual inspection approaches and conclude that "the most effective reading techniques in requirements, design, and coding phases are perspective-based reading, usage-based reading, and tool-assisted reading, respectively". Authors also concluded that most research seems to be based on data collected from academic, instead of industrial context.

In addition to being scarce, previous literature studies on code reviews have focused on topics that are quite specific. We argue that software engineering community would benefit from a broader understanding of themes covered in the code review literature. Therefore, the main objective of this study is to shed light on which themes can be identified in the research of code reviews. The exact research questions answered here is "what's the *focus* of the existing empirical articles on code reviews, software inspections, and code walkthroughs". In the rest of this article, we use the term *code review* to refer different review approaches (e.g., code reviews, software inspections, and code walkthroughs) We will answer our research question by conducting a systematic mapping study.

The goal of this mapping study, following the guidelines in [5], is to provide an overview of empirical research on code reviews, and identify the quantity and type of research, and results available within it. The results of this study can identify areas suitable for conducting systematic literature reviews [6], and areas where a primary study is more appropriate.

The rest of this paper is structured as follows. Section 2 gives an overview to our data collection. Section 3 presents our results. Section 4 provides an extended discussion regarding our findings and lists directions for future work. Section 5 describes limitations of this research. Finally, towards the end of the paper, Sect. 6 draws some conclusions.

2   Data Collection

2.1   Search for Primary Studies

The first phase of the study consisted of identifying primary studies from scientific databases. Search queries were defined to retrieve the initial selection of works to be filtered and screened later on. The search was carried out in the following digital libraries: IEEE (http://ieeexplore.ieee.org/Xplore/home.jsp), ACM (http://dl.acm.org/), and Scopus (https://www.scopus.com/).

The format of queries differs between platforms. Table 1 shows how queries were defined in each library. The actual search was conducted in June 2018; the Results-column in Table 1 indicates the number of hits in each platform.

In total, the queries produced a combined total of 1426 articles. This initial set of articles was then examined to remove duplicate articles. A total of 281 articles were removed automatically based on duplicate DOIs, leaving 1145 articles for further analysis.

Table 1. Executed queries for each digital library.

Database	Search	Results
IEEE	METADATA ONLY: ((("code review") OR "code inspection") OR "code walkthrough")	297
ACM	acmdlTitle:("code review" "code inspection" "code walkthrough") OR recordAbstract:("code review" "code inspection" "code walkthrough") OR keywords.author.keyword:("code review" "code inspection" "code walkthrough")	267
Scopus	(TITLE-ABS-KEY("code review") OR TITLE-ABS-KEY("code inspection") OR TITLE-ABS-KEY("code walkthrough")) AND (LIMIT-TO (DOCTYPE, "cp") OR LIMIT-TO (DOCTYPE, "ar") OR LIMIT-TO (DOCTYPE, "re")) AND (LIMIT-TO (SUBJAREA, "COMP") OR LIMIT-TO (SUBJAREA, "ENGI")) AND (LIMIT-TO (LANGUAGE, "English"))	862
Total		1426

2.2 Screening of Papers for Inclusion and Exclusion

The 1145 articles were screened based on their titles and abstracts. The application of inclusion and exclusion criteria to titles and abstracts was conducted by four researchers working in parallel. We were inclusive taking a paper to full-text reading when in doubt. The following criteria state when a study was excluded:

- Studies presenting tools that are not specifically about code reviews (e.g., tools for clone detection, tools for static code analysis).
- Studies not presented in English.
- Studies presenting summaries of conferences/editorials.
- Studies not accessible in full-text.
- Books and gray literature.
- Studies that are replications of other studies.

This exclusion phase led to removal of 622 articles.

2.3 Selecting Empirical Studies in the Software Engineering Field

After the initial screening and exclusion of non-relevant articles, 523 articles remained. These articles were then further inspected, including only articles that were from the field of software engineering, and provided empirical results related to code reviews. More precisely, the following inclusion criteria was applied: (1) Studies are in the field of software engineering, and (2) Studies present empirical results on code reviews (e.g. qualitative or quantitative data on code reviews). Opinion pieces without any data or where the focus was on something else than code reviews were excluded. This led to a final data set of 75 articles.

Most of the articles in our final data set have been published in conference proceedings (61%). 32% of the publications were journal articles and the remaining 7% were published in magazines and workshops.

3   Qualitative Content Analysis of Research Questions

For all the papers, we extracted excerpts describing the objectives, hypothesis and explicit research questions of the work. Some of the papers did not have any research questions and in some cases even the objectives were loosely defined. In these cases, we extracted excerpts from the conclusions that illustrated outcomes of the work. As the last option, if we failed to find illustrative excerpts, the main contributions of a paper we defined by our own words. In addition, for every paper, we extracted the context of code reviews (e.g. academic, industry, or open source software development). Some papers had multiple contexts, in which case all were recorded.

Next, we carried out a qualitative content analysis of research questions to identify themes of the research. First, one of the authors went through all the excerpts, and created a list of potential categories. At this phase, some of the excerpts were augmented by reading the original publication. Next, themes were discussed with an another author who also read the excerpts. This resulted in some themes to be merged and some new themes to be created. Finally, when all the papers were classified to potentially multiple categories, the categorization was finalized jointly by all the authors.

The final categories and the number of articles assigned to each category are the following. The list of papers in each category divided by the context is provided in Table 2; in our study, an article could be mapped to multiple categories.

Review Methods. This category is related to description, combination and comparison of different code review practices. Some of the studies are descriptive and focus on explaining (new) code review methods and best practices, as in [7]: "Building on the existing literature, here we add insights from a recent large-scale study of Microsoft developers' code review practices to summarize the challenges that code-change authors and reviewers face, suggest best code-reviewing practices, and discuss tradeoffs that practitioners should consider." Some papers in the category focus on (quantitative) comparison review methods as illustrate in the following excerpt of research hypothesis [8]: "There is significant difference in the number defects found by those subjects performing ad-hoc inspection and those performing systematic inspection of object oriented code". (33 papers)

Human Behaviour. Papers in this category focus on Individual differences between reviewers (e.g., "how effective developers are at conducting code reviews and the degree of variation among them" [9] and behaviour of individual reviewer, e.g., by using eye-tracking [10,11]. The category is often linked to the previous category of describing new review method and research questions such as "Do developers who are shown information that could potentially help avoid the introduction of bugs behave differently than without that information" [12] (15 papers)

Teamwork. Papers in this category focus on communication, team configurations and teamwork. Examples of research questions in this category are "Does the number of involved teams influence the effectiveness of distributed code review" [13] and "what do reviewers discuss in test code reviews" [14] In many cases, the role of teamwork was implicit while research questions were more broadly defined. (14 papers)

Outcome of Code Reviews. Papers in this category focus on effect of code reviews, for example, which kinds of errors are found or how many of the errors can be found. The category is closely linked to *review methods* category. Examples of research questions in category include "What is the impact of continuous code reviews and inspections on code quality, What are the most common bugs among the code written by sophomores? What are the most common code smells identified within the code written by sophomores?" [15] (14 papers)

Role of Code to be Reviewed. Papers in this category focus on the relation of reviews and code to be reviewed. How properties of code to be reviewed affect reviewing is more specific when compared to other categories, but it was still clearly emerging from the data. Excepts illustrating this category include "Does the number lines of code to be reviewed influence the effectiveness of distributed code review?" [13] and "What factors can influence how long it takes for a patch to be reviewed?" [16] (5 papers)

Reasons for Conducting Code Reviews. Papers in this category address explicitly the reasons or motivations for conducting code reviews, with research questions like "What are the motivations for code review at Google [...] How do Google developers perceive code review?" [17] (4 papers)

Table 2. Topical classification of papers. (*) Some papers use data from more than one context, for instance when comparing industry with academia.

Category	n	Context*	Papers
Review methods	33	industry (14), open source (3), academia (15), unclear (1), government (1), simulated review (1)	[1, 7, 8, 14, 17–45]
Human behaviour	15	industry (5), open source (3), academia (8)	[9–12, 46–56]
Teamwork	14	industry (9), open source (2), academia (3)	[7, 13, 14, 16, 24, 35, 57–64]
Outcome of code reviews	14	industry (5), open source (7), academia (2)	[15, 43, 49, 65–75]
Role of code to be reviewed	5	industry (1), open source (4)	[13, 14, 16, 76, 77]
Reasons for conducting code reviews	4	industry (2), academia (1), not defined (1)	[17, 78–80]

While reviews are considered somewhat classical technique, we identified only few studies published prior to mid-1990s. Publication year of the studies are illustrated in Fig. 1.

	1980	1990	2000	2010	2020
Review methods	1		4 2121 111 1	13	113144
Human behavior		1	1 1112	1	3121
Teamwork			22 21 1		2 112
Outcome of code reviews		1	1 1	1	22411
Role of code to be reviewed				1	211
Reasons for conducting code reviews			1	1	1 1
All	1	1 1	522232	232141141	639685

Fig. 1. The number of publication per year for each category (a single paper can be classified into multiple categories) and the total number of publications identified each year.

4   Discussion

The largest category of research topics identified in this mapping study, with 38% of papers related to it is description, combination and comparison of different code review practices. The category overlaps heavily with other categories, however. For example, description of a new code review approach is often related to analysis of how people behave when applying the new methods, and quantifying the results of code reviews.

Indeed, the second largest groups in our analysis are "Communication, team configurations and teamwork", " Effect of code reviews (e.g., which kinds of errors are found)", and "Individual differences and behavior of reviewers". Each of these themes to related to ca. 16% of all the papers.

Although we were able to identify many studies that either compare (effectiveness of) code review techniques or identify benefits of code review, there are only few studies that compare effectiveness of code reviews to other quality assurance techniques (e.g., [75]). We would like to see more studies that compare code reviews directly to alternative or complementary methods, such as test driven development or pair programming.

Three different contexts are common when considering reviews that contain empirical results – open source, industry, and education. Sometimes, they (partially) overlap or complement each other in the studies (hence the small mismatch in numbers per category and total in Table 2). In our study, ca. half of the studies have been conducted with students and novices. This is a significant improvement to earlier review by Ebad [4], where only four percent of the research was conducted in the industry context.

We are somewhat surprised by the fact that there are very few old articles with empirical evidence, although code reviews is considered a classic topic. Furthermore, these initial papers were really placing the focus on the essentials of code reviews as a quality assurance and bug-fixing instrument. Based on our study, mid-1990s seem to mark the point when there was increasing empirical interest in reviews in general, and only after 2010 there are several papers that empirically study reviews. Granted, the increasing interest in reviews has also meant that the research is more versatile, addressing various topics revolving around reviews but not necessarily studying their effectiveness as a mechanism for quality assurance.

Finally, we did not consider the evolution of the term code review in this study; however it is clear that the meaning of the term has evolved significantly. For example, in 1980s, the term 'software review' meant software inspection where the quality of a software module was inspected following a certain process [81], whereas today software review more often refers to the acceptance decision for inclusion of a contribution in an open source project [82]. Understanding this evolution is a topic for future work.

5   Limitations and Threats to Validity

There are multiple biases related to the selection of primary research. Retrospectively, the biggest selection choice we made in the paper was to exclude tool papers, where empirical evidence was focused on evaluating the tool. It is likely that in the process we also eliminated some data that also acts as evidence regarding code reviews more generally as well. By inspecting many of the tools papers as well, we came to a conclusion that in general they are not comparable to papers that are solely dedicated to code reviews. However, studying the tool perspective remains an possible direction for future work.

Another dimension we deliberately excluded in this study is the use of code reviews in education. Such studies take a very different stand to code reviews, and while they would have contributed to versatility of the mapping study in general, based on reading many of them, they might have resulted in a category of their own in the classification. Hence, we feel that they deserve a paper of their own. Publications that used educational context, but did not focus on how to teach code reviews were included, however.

The general limitations associated with any mapping study also apply to our work, including in particular bias in selection of the reviewed papers and inaccuracy in data extraction. Since we mainly relied on search engines to retrieve the primary studies, the search engines may have influenced the completeness of the identified studies. The extraction process may have also resulted in inaccuracies, even though the reviewers practiced extraction jointly. Quality assessment of studies in systematic reviews still remains a major problem [83].

6   Conclusions

Code inspections are a classic approach to quality assurance. Despite frequent use of the method in industry, there are only few systematic literature studies of the field. In this systematic mapping study we have illustrated what kinds of research themes can be identified in the code review literature.

The following themes emerged from analysis of 75 original articles: (1) description or comparison of different code review practices, (2) human behavior and differences between individual reviewers (3) communication and teamwork, (4) outcomes of code reviews, (5) how properties of code to be reviewed affect reviewing, and (6) reasons for conducting code reviews.

While many of the papers identified in this survey address effectiveness of code reviews, comparisons between code review to other approaches aiming to improve software quality are uncommon. Moreover, much of the knowledge is at least partially outdated due to the changes in software development and deployment methodologies. In contrast, softer issues, such as team behavior and participants roles in code review, have been gaining traction in research, resulting in various studies of code reviews from the socio-technical dimension.

While we acknowledge the importance of the socio-technical dimension, we believe that there is a need for further primary studies from purely technical point of view, taking code reviews as a quality assurance technique back into focus.

References

1. Myers, G.J.: A controlled experiment in program testing and code walk-throughs/inspections. Commun. ACM **21**(9), 760–768 (1978)
2. Bacchelli, A., Bird, C.: Expectations, outcomes, and challenges of modern code review. In: Proceedings of the 2013 International Conference on Software engineering, pp. 712–721. IEEE Press (2013)
3. Brykczynski, B.: A survey of software inspection checklists. ACM SIGSOFT Softw. Eng. Notes **24**(1), 82 (1999)
4. Ebad, S.: Inspection reading techniques applied to software artifacts-a systematic review. Comput. Syst. Sci. Eng. **32**(3), 213–226 (2017)
5. Petersen, K., Feldt, R., Mujtaba, S., Mattsson, M.: Systematic mapping studies in software engineering. In: Proc. of the 12th International Conference on Evaluation and Assessment in Software Engineering. EASE 2008, BCS Learning & Development, pp. 68–77 (2008)
6. Kitchenham, B.A., Charters, S.: Guidelines for performing systematic literature reviews in software engineering. Technical Report EBSE-2007-01, Keele Univ. (2007)
7. Greiler, M., Bird, C., Storey, M.A., MacLeod, L., Czerwonka, J.: Code reviewing in the trenches: Understanding challenges, best practices and tool needs (2016)
8. Dunsmore, A., Roper, M., Wood, M.: Systematic object-oriented inspection-an empirical study. In: Proceedings of the 23rd International Conference on Software Engineering, pp. 135–144. IEEE (2001)

9. Edmundson, A., Holtkamp, B., Rivera, E., Finifter, M., Mettler, A., Wagner, D.: An empirical study on the effectiveness of security code review. In: Jürjens, J., Livshits, B., Scandariato, R. (eds.) ESSoS 2013. LNCS, vol. 7781, pp. 197–212. Springer, Heidelberg (2013). https://doi.org/10.1007/978-3-642-36563-8_14

10. Begel, A., Vrzakova, H.: Eye movements in code review. In: Proceedings of the Workshop on Eye Movements in Programming, p. 5. ACM (2018)

11. Uwano, H., Nakamura, M., Monden, A., Matsumoto, K.I.: Analyzing individual performance of source code review using reviewers' eye movement. In: Proceedings of the 2006 Symposium on Eye Tracking Research & Applications, pp. 133–140. ACM (2006)

12. Foss, S.L., Murphy, G.C.: Do developers respond to code stability warnings? In: Proceedings of the 25th Annual International Conference on Computer Science and Software Engineering, pp. 162–170. IBM Corp. (2015)

13. dos Santos, E.W., Nunes, I.: Investigating the effectiveness of peer code review in distributed software development. In: Proceedings of the 31st Brazilian Symposium on Software Engineering, pp. 84–93. ACM (2017)

14. Spadini, D., Aniche, M., Storey, M.A., Bruntink, M., Bacchelli, A.: When testing meets code review: why and how developers review tests. In: 2018 IEEE/ACM 40th International Conference on Software Engineering (ICSE), pp. 677–687. IEEE (2018)

15. Sripada, S.K., Reddy, Y.R.: Code comprehension activities in undergraduate software engineering course-a case study. In: 24th Australasian Software Engineering Conference, vol. 2015, pp. 68–77. IEEE (2015)

16. Baysal, O., Kononenko, O., Holmes, R., Godfrey, M.W.: The influence of non-technical factors on code review. In: 2013 20th Working Conference on Reverse Engineering (WCRE), pp. 122–131. IEEE (2013)

17. Sadowski, C., Söderberg, E., Church, L., Sipko, M., Bacchelli, A.: Modern code review: a case study at google. In: Proceedings of the 40th International Conference on Software Engineering: Software Engineering in Practice, pp. 181–190. ACM (2018)

18. Fracz, W., Dajda, J.: Experimental validation of source code reviews on mobile devices. In: Gervasi, O., Murgante, B., Misra, S., Borruso, G., Torre, C.M., Rocha, A.M.A.C., Taniar, D., Apduhan, B.O., Stankova, E., Cuzzocrea, A. (eds.) ICCSA 2017. LNCS, vol. 10408, pp. 533–547. Springer, Cham (2017). https://doi.org/10.1007/978-3-319-62404-4_40

19. Baum, T., Leßmann, H., Schneider, K.: The choice of code review process: a survey on the state of the practice. In: Felderer, M., Méndez Fernández, D., Turhan, B., Kalinowski, M., Sarro, F., Winkler, D. (eds.) PROFES 2017. LNCS, vol. 10611, pp. 111–127. Springer, Cham (2017). https://doi.org/10.1007/978-3-319-69926-4_9

20. Ferreira, A.L., Machado, R.J., Silva, J.G., Batista, R.F., Costa, L., Paulk, M.C.: An approach to improving software inspections performance. In: 2010 IEEE International Conference on Software Maintenance, pp. 1–8. IEEE (2010)

21. Vassallo, C., Panichella, S., Palomba, F., Proksch, S., Zaidman, A., Gall, H.C.: Context is king: the developer perspective on the usage of static analysis tools. In: IEEE 25th International Conference on Software Analysis, Evolution and Reengineering (SANER), pp. 38–49. IEEE (2018)

22. Höst, M., Johansson, C.: Evaluation of code review methods through interviews and experimentation. J. Syst. Softw. **52**(2–3), 113–120 (2000)

23. Kamsties, E., Lott, C.M.: An empirical evaluation of three defect-detection techniques. In: Schäfer, W., Botella, P. (eds.) Software Engineering – ESEC 1995, pp. 362–383. Springer, Berlin (1995)

24. Müller, M.M.: Are reviews an alternative to pair programming? Empir. Softw. Eng. **9**(4), 335–351 (2004)
25. Khandelwal, S., Sripada, S.K., Reddy, Y.R.: Impact of gamification on code review process: an experimental study. In: Proceedings of the 10th Innovations in Software Engineering Conference, pp. 122–126. ACM (2017)
26. Hatton, L.: Testing the value of checklists in code inspections. IEEE Softw. **25**(4), 82–88 (2008)
27. Belli, F., Crisan, R.: Empirical performance analysis of computer-supported code-reviews. In: Proceedings The Eighth International Symposium on Software Reliability Engineering, pp. 245–255. IEEE (1997)
28. El Emam, K., Laitenberger, O.: Evaluating capture-recapture models with two inspectors. IEEE Trans. Softw. Eng. **27**(9), 851–864 (2001)
29. Hirao, T., Ihara, A., Matsumoto, K.I.: Pilot study of collective decision-making in the code review process. In: Proceedings of the 25th Annual International Conference on Computer Science and Software Engineering, pp. 248–251. IBM Corp (2015)
30. Olorisade, B.K., Vegas, S., Juristo, N.: Determining the effectiveness of three software evaluation techniques through informal aggregation. Inf. Softw. Technol. **55**(9), 1590–1601 (2013)
31. Runeson, P., Stefik, A., Andrews, A., Gronblom, S., Porres, I., Siebert, S.: A comparative analysis of three replicated experiments comparing inspection and unit testing. In: Second International Workshop on Replication in Empirical Software Engineering Research, vol. 2011, pp. 35–42. IEEE (2011)
32. De Vreede, G.J., Koneri, P.G., Dean, D.L., Fruhling, A.L., Wolcott, P.: A collaborative software code inspection: the design and evaluation of a repeatable collaboration process in the field. Int. J. Coop. Inf. Syst. **15**(02), 205–228 (2006)
33. Hémeury, B.: Report on the VERA experiment. In: González Harbour, M., de la Puente, J.A. (eds.) Ada-Europe 1999. LNCS, vol. 1622, pp. 103–113. Springer, Heidelberg (1999). https://doi.org/10.1007/3-540-48753-0_9
34. Kelly, D., Shepard, T.: Qualitative observations from software code inspection experiments. In: Proceedings of the 2002 conference of the Centre for Advanced Studies on Collaborative research, p. 5. IBM Press (2002)
35. Porter, A.A., Siy, H.P., Toman, C.A., Votta, L.G.: An experiment to assess the cost-benefits of code inspections in large scale software development. IEEE Trans. Softw. Eng. **23**(6), 329–346 (1997)
36. Wang, Y.Q., Qi, Z.Y., Zhang, L.J., Song, M.J.: Research and practice on education of SQA at source code level. Int. J. Eng. Educ. **27**(1), 70 (2011)
37. Panko, R.R.: Applying code inspection to spreadsheet testing. J. Manage. Inf. Syst. **16**(2), 159–176 (1999)
38. Koneri, P.G., de Vreede, G.-J., Dean, D.L., Fruhling, A.L., Wolcott, P.: The design and field evaluation of a repeatable collaborative software code inspection process. In: Fukś, H., Lukosch, S., Salgado, A.C. (eds.) CRIWG 2005. LNCS, vol. 3706, pp. 325–340. Springer, Heidelberg (2005). https://doi.org/10.1007/11560296_26
39. Cristia, M., Frydman, C.: Formal and semi-formal verification of a web voting system. Int. J. Web Inf. Syst. **11**(2), 183–204 (2015)
40. da Silva Neto, A.V., Vismari, L.F., Gimenes, R.A.V., Sesso, D.B., de Almeida, J.R., Cugnasca, P.S., Camargo, J.B.: A practical analytical approach to increase confidence in pld-based systems safety analysis. IEEE Syst. J. 99, 1–12 (2017)

41. Wood, M., Roper, M., Brooks, A., Miller, J.: Comparing and combining software defect detection techniques: a replicated empirical study. In: Jazayeri, M., Schauer, H. (eds.) ESEC/SIGSOFT FSE -1997. LNCS, vol. 1301, pp. 262–277. Springer, Heidelberg (1997). https://doi.org/10.1007/3-540-63531-9_19

42. Wilkerson, J.W., Nunamaker, J.F., Mercer, R.: Comparing the defect reduction benefits of code inspection and test-driven development. IEEE Trans. Softw. Eng. **38**(3), 547–560 (2011)

43. Morales, R., McIntosh, S., Khomh, F.: Do code review practices impact design quality? a case study of the qt, vtk, and itk projects. In: IEEE 22nd International Conference on Software Analysis, Evolution, and Reengineering (SANER), pp. 171–180 IEEE (2015)

44. Oliveira, R., Estácio, B., Garcia, A., Marczak, S., Prikladnicki, R., Kalinowski, M., Lucena, C.: Identifying code smells with collaborative practices: a controlled experiment. In: X Brazilian Symposium on Software Components, Architectures and Reuse (SBCARS), pp. 61–70. IEEE 2016 (2016)

45. Swamidurai, R., Dennis, B., Kannan, U.: Investigating the impact of peer code review and pair programming on test-driven development. In: IEEE SOUTHEAST-CON 2014, pp. 1–5. IEEE (2014)

46. Bisant, D.B., Lyle, J.R.: A two-person inspection method to improve programming productivity. IEEE Trans. Softw. Eng. **10**, 1294–1304 (1989)

47. McMeekin, D.A., von Konsky, B.R., Chang, E., Cooper, D.J.A.: Measuring cognition levels in collaborative processes for software engineering code inspections. In: Ulieru, M., Palensky, P., Doursat, R. (eds.) IT Revolutions 2008. LNICST, vol. 11, pp. 32–43. Springer, Heidelberg (2009). https://doi.org/10.1007/978-3-642-03978-2_5

48. McMeekin, D.A., von Konsky, B.R., Chang, E., Cooper, D.J.: Checklist based reading's influence on a developer's understanding. In: 19th Australian Conference on Software Engineering (aswec 2008), pp. 489–496. IEEE (2008)

49. McIntosh, S., Kamei, Y., Adams, B., Hassan, A.E.: An empirical study of the impact of modern code review practices on software quality. Empir. Softw. Eng. **21**(5), 2146–2189 (2016)

50. Stålhane, T., Awan, T.H.: Improving the software inspection process. In: Richardson, I., Abrahamsson, P., Messnarz, R. (eds.) EuroSPI 2005. LNCS, vol. 3792, pp. 163–174. Springer, Heidelberg (2005). https://doi.org/10.1007/11586012_16

51. Dunsmore, A., Roper, M., Wood, M.: The role of comprehension in software inspection. J. Syst. Softw. **52**(2–3), 121–129 (2000)

52. Da Cunha, A.D., Greathead, D.: Does personality matter?: an analysis of code-review ability. Commun. ACM **50**(5), 109–112 (2007)

53. Thongtanunam, P., McIntosh, S., Hassan, A.E., Iida, H.: Investigating code review practices in defective files: an empirical study of the qt system. In: Proceedings of the 12th Working Conference on Mining Software Repositories, pp. 168–179. IEEE (2015)

54. Kononenko, O., Baysal, O., Guerrouj, L., Cao, Y., Godfrey, M.W.: Investigating code review quality: do people and participation matter? In: 2015 IEEE International Conference on Software Maintenance and Evolution (ICSME), pp. 111–120. IEEE (2015)

55. de Mello, R.M., Oliveira, R.F., Garcia, A.F.: On the influence of human factors for identifying code smells: a multi-trial empirical study. In: ACM/IEEE International Symposium on Empirical Software Engineering and Measurement (ESEM), vol. 2017, pp. 68–77. IEEE (2017)

56. Murakami, Y., Tsunoda, M., Uwano, H.: Wap: does reviewer age affect code review performance? In: IEEE 28th International Symposium on Software Reliability Engineering (ISSRE), vol. 2017, pp. 164–169. IEEE (2017)

57. Seaman, C.B., Basili, V.R.: An empirical study of communication in code inspections. In: Proceedings of the (19th) International Conference on Software Engineering, pp. 96–106. IEEE (1997)

58. Porter, A., Siy, H., Mockus, A., Votta, L.: Understanding the sources of variation in software inspections. ACM Trans. Softw. Eng. Methodol. **7**(1), 41–79 (1998)

59. Müller, M.M.: Two controlled experiments concerning the comparison of pair programming to peer review. J. Syst. Softw. **78**(2), 166–179 (2005)

60. Spohrer, K., Kude, T., Schmidt, C.T., Heinzl, A.: Knowledge creation in information systems development teams: The role of pair programming and peer code review. In: ECIS. 213 (2013)

61. Miller, J., Yin, Z.: A cognitive-based mechanism for constructing software inspection teams. IEEE Trans. Softw. Eng. **30**(11), 811–825 (2004)

62. Sutherland, A., Venolia, G.: Can peer code reviews be exploited for later information needs? In: 2009 31st International Conference on Software Engineering-Companion Volume, pp. 259–262. IEEE (2009)

63. Seaman, C.B., Basili, V.R.: Communication and organization: An empirical study of discussion in inspection meetings. IEEE Trans. Softw. Eng. **24**(7), 559–572 (1998)

64. Bosu, A., Carver, J.C., Bird, C., Orbeck, J., Chockley, C.: Process aspects and social dynamics of contemporary code review: Insights from open source development and industrial practice at microsoft. IEEE Trans. Softw. Eng. **43**(1), 56–75 (2016)

65. Panichella, S., Arnaoudova, V., Di Penta, M., Antoniol, G.: Would static analysis tools help developers with code reviews? In: IEEE 22nd International Conference on Software Analysis, Evolution, and Reengineering (SANER), pp. 161–170. IEEE (2015)

66. Thompson, C., Wagner, D.: A large-scale study of modern code review and security in open source projects. In: Proceedings of the 13th International Conference on Predictive Models and Data Analytics in Software Engineering, pp. 83–92. ACM (2017)

67. Lei, Q., He, Z., Fuqun, H., Bin, L.: Classification of air on-board software code defects and investigations. Procedia Eng. **15**, 3577–3583 (2011)

68. Russell, G.W.: Experience with inspection in ultralarge-scale development. IEEE Softw. **8**(1), 25–31 (1991)

69. Siy, H., Votta, L.: Does the modern code inspection have value? In: Proceedings of the IEEE International Conference on Software- Maintenance (ICSM 2001), p. 281. IEEE (2001)

70. Bavota, G., Russo, B.: Four eyes are better than two: On the impact of code reviews on software quality. In: 2015 IEEE International Conference on Software Maintenance and Evolution (ICSME), pp. 81–90. IEEE (2015)

71. Bosu, A., Carver, J.C.: Impact of peer code review on peer impression formation: a survey. In: ACM/IEEE International Symposium on Empirical Software Engineering and Measurement, vol. 2013, p. 133–142. IEEE (2013)

72. Beller, M., Bacchelli, A., Zaidman, A., Juergens, E.: Modern code reviews in open-source projects: which problems do they fix? In: Proceedings of the 11th Working Conference on Mining Software Repositories, pp. 202–211. ACM (2014)

73. Bernhart, M., Grechenig, T.: On the understanding of programs with continuous code reviews. In: 2013 21st International Conference on Program Comprehension (ICPC), pp. 192–198. IEEE (2013)
74. Mäntylä, M.V., Lassenius, C.: What types of defects are really discovered in code reviews? IEEE Trans. Softw. Eng. **35**(3), 430–448 (2008)
75. Runeson, P., Stefik, A., Andrews, A.: Variation factors in the design and analysis of replicated controlled experiments. Empir. Softw. Eng. **19**(6), 1781–1808 (2014)
76. Baysal, O., Kononenko, O., Holmes, R., Godfrey, M.W.: Investigating technical and non-technical factors influencing modern code review. Empir. Softw. Eng. **21**(3), 932–959 (2016)
77. Nanthaamornphong, A., Chaisutanon, A.: Empirical evaluation of code smells in open source projects: preliminary results. In: Proceedings of the 1st International Workshop on Software Refactoring, pp. 5–8. ACM (2016)
78. Perry, D.E., Porter, A., Wade, M.W., Votta, L.G., Perpich, J.: Reducing inspection interval in large-scale software development. IEEE Trans. Softw. Eng. **28**(7), 695–705 (2002)
79. Jenkins, G.L., Ademoye, O.: Can individual code reviews improve solo programming on an introductory course? Innov. Teach. Learn. Inf. Comput. Sci. **11**(1), 71–79 (2012)
80. Baum, T., Liskin, O., Niklas, K., Schneider, K.: Factors influencing code review processes in industry. In: Proceedings of the 2016 24th ACM SIGSOFT International Symposium on Foundations of Software Engineering, pp. 85–96. ACM (2016)
81. Ackerman, A.F., Buchwald, L.S., Lewski, F.H.: Software inspections: an effective verification process. IEEE Softw. **6**(3), 31–36 (1989)
82. Rigby, P., Cleary, B., Painchaud, F., Storey, M.A., German, D.: Contemporary peer review in action: lessons from open source development. IEEE Softw. **29**(6), 56–61 (2012)
83. Kitchenham, B., Brereton, P.: A systematic review of systematic review process research in software engineering. Inf. Softw. Technol. **55**(12), 2049–2075 (2013)

Optimising Analytical Software Quality Assurance

Stefan Wagner(✉)

Institute of Software Technology, University of Stuttgart, Stuttgart, Germany
stefan.wagner@iste.uni-stuttgart.de

Abstract. While optimising quality assurance has been an important research area for many years, we still see interesting new ideas in this area such as incorporating psychological factors, detecting pseudo-tested code and detecting code with low fault risk.

Keywords: Quality assurance · Optimisation · Economics · Test suite optimisation

1 Optimisation of Quality Assurance

Analytical quality assurance is the part of software quality assurance that analyses artefacts and processes to assess the level of quality and identify quality shortcomings. Analytical quality assurance is a major cost factor in any software development project. While real numbers are hard to find, any practitioner would agree that they spend a lot of time on testing and similar activities. At the same time, analytical quality assurance is indispensable to avoid quality problems of all kinds.

Hence, we have a set of activities in the development process that are expensive but are also decisive for the quality, and thereby probably the success, of a software product. Therefore, it is a practical need to optimise what kinds of analytical quality assurance are employed, to what degree and with how much effort to reach high quality and low costs.

In the following, we will first discuss how this problem could be framed from an economics point of view. Second, we will discuss the progress on evaluating and understanding the effectiveness and efficiency of various analytical quality assurance techniques. Third, we the will widen our perspective by discussing psychological aspects of quality assurance, and, finally, discuss some concrete, current proposals to optimise software testing.

2 Quality Economics

As the optimisation of quality assurance contains many different factors such as the effort spent for the techniques and what kind of techniques, what kind of

D. Winkler et al. (Eds.): SWQD 2020, LNBIP 371, pp. 134–138, 2020.
https://doi.org/10.1007/978-3-030-35510-4_9

faults are in the software it is difficult to find a common unit. Hence, various quality economics approaches have been proposed that use monetary units [1, 10].

We have proposed a quality economics model to estimate and evaluate costs and revenue from using analytical quality assurance mainly based on effort and difficulty functions of faults and quality assurance techniques [11–13]. We show in Fig. 1 just the part of the model describing the direct costs of applying an analytical quality assurance technique. Such an application usually comes with some kind of fixed setup costs, execution costs depending on how much effort we spend and removal costs depending on the probability that we detect a given fault.

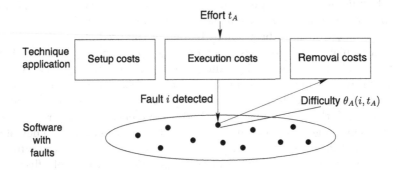

Fig. 1. The direct costs of an analytical quality assurance technique

This needs to be complemented with future costs describing the costs incurred by faults not detected by analytical quality assurance but leading to failures in the field. Those faults need also to be removed and there are further effect costs such as compensations to the customers. We showed that especially the latter are an important part of the model, but it is extremely difficult to determine. A very simple fault can have catastrophic effects while a very complicated, far ranging fault might never lead to a failure. Overall, we found that the empirical basis is too thin to practical apply such models and, because of the difficulty of collecting all the necessary data, might never improve.

3   Effectiveness and Efficiency of Quality Assurance Techniques

Therefore, we are convinced that it is more useful to rather devote research on the effectiveness (what share of the faults is found?) and efficiency (what is the relation of the number of found faults to effort spent?) of particular quality assurance techniques to at least be able to judge and compare them to have a basis for the decision what techniques to apply when and for what. There have been many studies for evaluating these aspects for various quality assurance techniques. In particular testing and inspections have been a focus of empirical research.

We have also contributed to better understand several quality assurance techniques. For model-based testing, we could show that a large share of the detected defects are already found during the modelling activity. The created test suite itself was not more effective than a test suite created by experts but was able to find other defects, often defects that require a particular long interaction sequence [9]. For black-box integration testing, we could show that test suites with a higher data-flow-based coverage are able to detect more more defects [2].

In a comparison of tests, reviews and automated static analysis [15], we found that automated static analysis finds a subset of defect types of reviews, but if it detected a specific type, it would detect it more thoroughly. Tests found completely different detect types than reviews and automated static analysis. In a study only of automated static analysis [14], we found that none of the analysed 72 field defects would have been found by one of the used static analysis tools. For the particular static analysis technique clone detection, we found that by looking particularly at clones with differences between their instance, we found 107 faults in five production systems leading to the observation that every other clone with unintended differences between its instances constitutes a fault [3].

Together with the large and growing body of evidence from other researchers, this starts to give a good understanding of the effectiveness and efficiency of analytical quality assurance. The main weaknesses I see still today is the infrequent replication of studies and slightly different operationalisations of effectiveness and efficiency that make meta-analysis difficult.

4   Psychological Aspects

A further dimension we believe to be of critical importance but that has not widely been investigated are psychological factors of the software developers and testers applying analytical quality assurance. In particular, we studied the use of automated static analysis in relation to the personality of the developers [8] and the stress it caused for developers [7]. For example, we found that while people with a high level of agreeableness show a relatively structured strategy in dealing with static analysis findings by working with small changes in cycles, people with high neuroticism show a more chaotic approach by making larger changes and impulsive decisions: They change the file they were working on without finishing the work they had started. Such findings can in turn inform how to improve quality assurance techniques or the user interfaces of corresponding tools.

5   Test Optimisation

Especially for the optimisation of tests, there is a lot of existing research on test case prioritisation and test suite minimisation. These techniques aim at only executing relevant test cases and executing test cases with a high probability of detecting a defect for a giving change early. Yet, there is still room for improvement. We recently introduced two novel concepts to optimise test suites: (1) detection of pseudo-tested code [4,6] and (2) inverse defect prediction [5].

We define *pseudo-tested* code as code that is covered by some test case but the test case does not effectively test that code. It would not detect faults in that code. We detect pseudo-tested code by using an extreme mutation operator: We remove the whole implementation of a method or function and return a constant. In empirical analyses, we found in all 19 study objects that pseudo-tested code existed and that the median of pseudo-tested methods was 10%. It can help in a practical setting to reduce incorrect coverage values to concentrate on test cases that effectively add more coverage.

We introduced *inverse defect detection* to identify methods that are too trivial to be tested. For example, many getter and setter methods in Java contain only trivial functionality. In many cases, it is not time and effort well spent to test these methods. We identified a set of metrics that we considered to be likely indicators for trivial methods. We used these for association rule mining and identified association rules to identify methods that have a low fault risk. This forms effectively a theory for low-fault-risk methods. The predictor that uses these rules is what we call inverse defect detection. It is effective in identifying methods with low fault risk: On average, only 0.3% of the methods classified as ?low fault risk? are faulty. The identified methods are, on average, 5.7 times less likely to contain a fault than an arbitrary method in the analysed systems. Hence, we can either not test those methods at all or at least execute the corresponding test cases last.

6   Conclusions

Optimising analytical quality assurance has been an important practical problem as well as a corresponding research area for many years. We have learnt that precise economical models suffer from the lack of empirical data and, hence, have not led to much practical progress. Yet, many empirical studies contributed to a better understanding of the effectiveness and efficiency of particular quality assurance methods. Furthermore, new research directions such as the influence of psychological factors, pseudo-tested code and the prediction of low-fault-risk code provide us with more theoretical understanding and already practical impact in the form of new tools.

References

1. Boehm, B.W., Huang, L., Jain, A., Madachy, R.J.: The ROI of software dependability: the iDAVE model. IEEE Softw. **21**(3), 54–61 (2004)
2. Hellhake, D., Schmid, T., Wagner, S.: Using data flow-based coverage criteria for black-box integration testing of distributed software systems. In: 12th IEEE Conference on Software Testing, Validation and Verification, ICST 2019, Xi'an, China, 22–27 April 2019, pp. 420–429. IEEE (2019)
3. Jürgens, E., Deissenboeck, F., Hummel, B., Wagner, S.: Do code clones matter? In: Proceedings of 31st International Conference on Software Engineering, ICSE 2009, Vancouver, Canada, 16–24 May 2009, pp. 485–495. IEEE (2009)

4. Niedermayr, R., Jürgens, E., Wagner, S.: Will my tests tell me if I break this code? In: Proceedings of the International Workshop on Continuous Software Evolution and Delivery, CSED@ICSE 2016, Austin, Texas, USA, 14–22 May 2016, pp. 23–29. ACM (2016)

5. Niedermayr, R., Röhm, T., Wagner, S.: Too trivial to test? An inverse view on defect prediction to identify methods with low fault risk. PeerJ Comput. Sci. **5**, e187 (2019)

6. Niedermayr, R., Wagner, S.: Is the stack distance between test case and method correlated with test effectiveness? In Ali, S., Garousi, V. (eds.) Proceedings of the Evaluation and Assessment on Software Engineering, EASE 2019, Copenhagen, Denmark, 15–17 April 2019, pp. 189–198. ACM (2019)

7. Ostberg, J., Wagner, S.: At ease with your warnings: the principles of the salutogenesis model applied to automatic static analysis. In: IEEE 23rd International Conference on Software Analysis, Evolution, and Reengineering, SANER 2016, Suita, Osaka, Japan, 14–18 March 2016, vol. 1, pp. 629–633. IEEE Computer Society (2016)

8. Ostberg, J., Wagner, S., Weilemann, E.: Does personality influence the usage of static analysis tools?: an explorative experiment. In: Proceedings of the 9th International Workshop on Cooperative and Human Aspects of Software Engineering, CHASE@ICSE 2016, Austin, Texas, USA, 16 May 2016, p. 75–81. ACM (2016)

9. Pretschner, A., Prenninger, W., Wagner, S., Kühnel, C., Baumgartner, M., Sostawa, B., Zölch, R., Stauner, T.: One evaluation of model-based testing and its automation. In: Roman, G., Griswold, W.G., Nuseibeh, B. (eds.) 27th International Conference on Software Engineering (ICSE 2005), St. Louis, Missouri, USA, 15–21 May 2005, pp. 392–401. ACM (2005)

10. Slaughter, S., Harter, D.E., Krishnan, M.S.: Evaluating the cost of software quality. Commun. ACM **41**(8), 67–73 (1998)

11. Wagner, S.: A literature survey of the quality economics of defect-detection techniques. In: Travassos, G.H., Maldonado, J.C., Wohlin, C. (eds.) 2006 International Symposium on Empirical Software Engineering (ISESE 2006), Rio de Janeiro, Brazil, 21–22 September 2006, pp. 194–203. ACM (2006)

12. Wagner, S.: A model and sensitivity analysis of the quality economics of defect-detection techniques. In Pollock, L.L., Pezzè, M. (eds.) Proceedings of the ACM/SIGSOFT International Symposium on Software Testing and Analysis, ISSTA 2006, Portland, Maine, USA, 17–20 July 2006, pp. 73–84. ACM (2006)

13. Wagner, S.: Cost optimisation of analytical software quality assurance. Ph.D. thesis, Technical University Munich, Germany (2007)

14. Wagner, S., Deissenboeck, F., Aichner, M., Wimmer, J., Schwalb, M.: An evaluation of two bug pattern tools for Java. In: First International Conference on Software Testing, Verification, and Validation, ICST 2008, Lillehammer, Norway, 9–11 April 2008, pp. 248–257. IEEE Computer Society (2008)

15. Wagner, S., Jürjens, J., Koller, C., Trischberger, P.: Comparing bug finding tools with reviews and tests. In: Khendek, F., Dssouli, R. (eds.) TestCom 2005. LNCS, vol. 3502, pp. 40–55. Springer, Heidelberg (2005). https://doi.org/10.1007/11430230_4

Author Index

Printed in the United States
By Bookmasters